This is the story of Bosworth Acad college that has been on a ten-year journey to transform their culture. As I read about their joyful, yet rigorous approach to learning, to community, to beautiful work all assessed through close attention to global competencies, I became increasingly inspired and filled with hope. I encourage you to read this, to listen to the young people, staff colleagues, and community members as they describe the vibrant, agentic work of their college. Highly recommended - strong on vision, strong on detail - a winning combination.

Dame Alison Peacock
Chief Executive
Chartered College of Teaching

This is an inspiring book, not just because of its clear moral intent that is then translated into school action, but because it draws on a comprehensive set of individual contributions across the academy – a real learning community. In all our work we have challenged the top-down approach to school improvement, knowing that you must engage the whole school community to this common purpose. And by improvement we mean education of the whole child, building up their agency and self-confidence. Very often schools are closed to their community and yet we know our young people's aspirations and self-belief are often tied to it. I applaud how this book shares this mission and makes the

challenge real and doable in all contexts.

John Baumber
Head of International Centre for Educational Enhancement
University of Bolton

This book expertly curates stories from the learning communities that together make up Bosworth Academy. It weaves together the voices of students and staff to let them explain to you for themselves how the Fourth Way has impacted their lives. At Whole Education, we believe in the power of networks and storytelling to surface the answers to questions that our schools and communities are trying to answer. In this book, we see the potential to share the power of networks that exists in one community for the benefit of those beyond that community. We are certain that others will read the stories and be inspired to think of how they might shape the unwritten stories of their own communities.

Shonogh Pilgrim
Head of Secondary
The Whole Education Network

I remember very clearly, my first visit to Bosworth Academy, and how impressed I was by the school's commitment to the Fourth Way, at a time, as intimated in the introduction, when Bosworth was swimming against the tide. We are delighted, as an organisation, to feature in Neely Gale's piece on student agency. This is because the power of student agency is something to which we are committed as an education charity, and it is also a power that Bosworth has harnessed and used to drive forward its Fourth Way. The academy trusts its school and the local community to know what's right in terms of the education of its students. Bosworth Academy has been brave and proved to be right.

Miranda Perry,
Director of World Class Schools Quality Mark

Good things take time and this book describes time well spent to produce something of worth: a learning experience that is designed to engage with youngsters. Bosworth Academy has explored every avenue to design a coherent and demanding curriculum and then to teach it well. There is much in this book of benefit to any school.

Mick Waters

With the demise of the Community College, the school became cut off from the community. It was physically on the edge of the village and people had no reason to visit unless they had children studying there.

Thankfully, that changed again and the school's relationship with the village has greatly improved. Much of the change has been due to the decision to adopt the principles of the Fourth Way and put them into practice as part of the student's everyday experience, not just as an add-on.

Extract from 'Bosworth Academy in the Community'
By Pat and Colin Crane
Community Leaders

Acknowledgement

This book is dedicated to our entire learning community - the premises officers, cleaning staff, support staff, parents, governors, educational networks, and the local community. Without you, none of the work described in this book would have been possible.

The School of the Fourth Way

Preparing students for the test of life,
not a life of tests

Written by the staff and students of Bosworth Academy

Foreword by Andy Hargreaves

In January of 2014, not far short of a decade ago, a letter arrived in my email inbox, seemingly from out of the blue. It read as follows:

Dear Dr. Hargreaves

I am an Assistant Principal at Bosworth Academy (one of the old Leicestershire Community Colleges you refer to in The Fourth Way).

I have been inspired by your work to create a long-term vision for our school, which has been enthusiastically approved by the Senior Leadership Team and the school Governors. We are set to launch this to the whole staff in June this year. Would you be interested in seeing this work and possibly helping us to improve it?

I look forward to hearing from you.

Regards
Dave Claricoates.

To be honest, I had no idea what to make of this letter. It could have been a prelude to a request for an endorsement for some forthcoming publication or other. If it was, this would turn out to be an 8-year prelude – surely, one of the longest in history. It could have been from somebody doing a leadership qualification or Masters' degree who was about to inflict an unwanted innovation on his school as a project, and who was seeking spurious backing from an expert in his support. But this was far from being the case. More likely, it could have been from a genuinely enthusiastic innovator who was nonetheless an outsider in his own school; eager for change himself but disconnected from colleagues who had learned over many years to be more sceptical. Yet, while Dave Claricoates's vision started with him, it didn't stay in his own head or even in the school's governors' heads for long.

Over many years, on and off, we have communicated back and forth, and Dave has kept me and my co-author, Dennis Shirley, periodically updated about Bosworth Academy and its progress. We have not succeeded in getting Dennis or me into the school yet. Living in North America hasn't made this easy, and possible appointments have been confounded by school holidays coinciding with my visits to the UK, by a long coast-to-coast hike that I was unsuccessful in finding a way to interrupt, and, of course, by the worst pandemic in a century.

But throughout all this time, Dave and the staff at Bosworth Academy have kept us apprised of their innovations, successes and, admirably, setbacks too. There is no innovation without failures along the way and acknowledging them and learning from them is a vital skill set in making educational change. But mostly, what Bosworth Academy has been achieving is impressive success, not in the abstract, but in moving towards realizing an inspiring and inclusive vision for the school and the community in very practical terms.

There are many risks in becoming an innovative school. Let's just look at six of them and how Bosworth Academy has responded.

1. The innovation is locked up in the head of one person. Only they understand it. They have the big picture. Everyone else gets a big binder. Dave Claricoates certainly has an expansive and inspiring vision. It has been charted out in impressive statements and elaborate curriculum charts. Before COVID-19, the Whole Education Network was still wondering, in its review of Bosworth Academy, if the whole school had yet grasped the full scope of what Dave and some of his management colleagues were desiring. This book shows, however, that the vision belongs to the many now, not the few. Students, teachers of different subjects, educators of different generations, and iconic community leaders all grasp the significance of what they believe a Fourth Way school might look like.

2. The innovation is a flash in the pan. It glitters and shines for a short period and then disappears. The people who participate are like Robert De Niro in Awakenings – roused from a long professional slumber, only to fall back to sleep again after a brief yet fragile period realizing what else might have been possible. But Bosworth Academy's innovative accomplishments are no flash in the pan. It's more than 8 years since I received my letter out of the blue and the school is still moving relentlessly forward. On May 10, 2014, one of my periodic communications from Dave Claricoates mentioned the following:

Our community focus has led us into the complicated world of local politics, and we are working to save the local library from closure and convert it into a community learning hub.

This library has not just survived but is now thriving with the help of local volunteers including pupils from the school, one of many projects that have been pursued with tenacity.

3. The innovation is not owned by the school, but rented from somewhere else – a hand-me-down curriculum, a digital technology platform, or the ideas of a famous expert, perhaps. Dennis Shirley and I are honoured and humbled, of course, by Bosworth Academy's adoption of Fourth Way principles to guide it growth and development. Yet we also admire how Bosworth has reached out to other frameworks as well as our own to provoke its thinking – including Michael Fullan's 6C's of deep learning, and the Organization for Economic Cooperation and Development's global competencies. Bosworth Academy has not just added these together, but it has integrated them in ways that many members of the school can effortlessly recall and recite. Bosworth's vision and culture belong to Bosworth - stimulated and supported by external ideas, but also fully rooted in the culture and history of Bosworth itself.

4. The innovation is a confusion of disparate and desperate interventions. Struggling schools, schools that have lost their way, or schools that have hit a plateau sometimes grasp at any and every opportunity that comes their way in a sincere but frantic effort to turn things around or change the game. Funds for all kinds of projects come into the school but they

feel disconnected and can often start to fight with each other for leaders' attention. Teachers get overwhelmed as sincere efforts start to fly off in all directions. As this book shows, a lot has been happening at Bosworth – the explorations of the forest, the library project, the Hereswode Games (less grisly than The Hunger Games, thankfully), the RealLife curriculum, and, my favourite, the Henrichment project. These many initiatives are bound together by clear philosophical principles, though, of truly personalized (rather than just digitally customized) learning, holistic education, authentic connections to the community, the value of pupil voice, and so on.

5. The innovation is defeated by external forces that undermine it. Many innovations fail or never even get off the ground, because the Grim Reaper of standardization and testing smothers them to death. Bosworth has never let the worst sides of the national policy environment quash its spirit or defeat its efforts. It has used significant workarounds like the A-level project-based learning courses. It has joined groups like the Whole Education Network to find solidarity in a common cause. Eventually, by staying out in front of policy rather than meekly following it, it has seen policy and especially Ofsted move in its direction of deeper and more innovative learning, rather than vice versa.

6. The innovation exiles itself from the school's own past. Innovators, especially those in the digital domain, too often disvalue what schools have accomplished before, writing their traditions off as outdated remnants of a long-gone factory age of education. But Bosworth educators and their students make many connections to a recent and distant past.

They show that Leicester Forest is a lot more than an M1 service station. It is a piece of geography and history that has deep roots in and connections to the community and that pupils now walk and run through to find out for themselves. And Bosworth Academy self-consciously sees itself as reinventing the proud tradition of Leicestershire Community Colleges that once offered inspiring leadership to secondary schools all over the country, half a century ago.

When Dennis Shirley and I brought what we called a Fourth Way into being, we didn't want schools to be crushed with tests or seduced by markets and brands. And we didn't want them to just go back to an age of disconnected and ultimately ineffective innovation, either. In different parts of the world, including England, we saw glimpses of something different and better that a global narrative of testing and technology for its own sake was leaving behind.

In the past 7 years, with colleagues, I have built on some of these principles to create a global network of education Ministers, senior civil servants, and professional leaders, that promotes humanistic values of broad excellence, equity, inclusion, well-being, democracy, and human rights. Our ARC Education Collaboratory of countries including Scotland, Ireland, Wales, and Iceland, as well as two Canadian provinces, periodically brings together senior leaders to advance these values with and for each other. During that time, we have seen the world start to move away from obsessions with testing and achievement comparisons, to something more inclusive too, like OECD's global competencies and the UN's sustainable development goals. We have achieved a lot together in this movement. But at the end of the day, it is schools that must show the way forward. Bosworth Academy has been doing just that – and then some! Please read the contributions of the many different contributors to this book from this school and its community. It will send shivers down your spine and put warmth into your soul.

Andy Hargreaves
Ottawa, Canada
November 2022

Introduction

In 2013 we came across a book called 'The Fourth Way' (1) by Andy Hargreaves and Dennis Shirley. The book was written in 2009 and set out a comprehensive approach to educational change which incorporated the best practices in global education since the 1960s as well as new approaches for the 21st century.

We were so inspired by the book that we thought we would try to turn our own school (Bosworth Academy in Leicestershire, England) into a fourth-way school. We contacted Andy Hargreaves, who kindly offered his support and has been very generous with his time ever since. In this book, we describe the 10-year journey we have been on to achieve this goal and to transform our school.

The Fourth Way segmented previous educational eras into three 'ways'. The first way was the early years of comprehensive education. It was a time of great innovation (particularly in community colleges like ours) but also of great unevenness where students could receive a very different quality of educational experience. In England, this 'way' lasted until the election of Margaret Thatcher in 1979.

The second way saw the introduction of market-based reforms in schools. Standardisation and quality control were achieved through the introduction of the National Curriculum in 1988 and Ofsted in 1992. Industrial-style targets were set for school performance - particularly around exam results. This period saw far greater consistency in educational provision but also a suffocating conformity - everyone having to do three-part lessons for example, even when it wasn't really appropriate. By all accounts, even the inventor of the three-part lesson complained he didn't mean for them to be used all the time!

Tony Blair's election win in 1997 with New Labour heralded his famous 'Third Way' approach. This saw increased investment in schools (particularly the buildings) but also increased pressure on schools to meet centrally set targets. Schools were encouraged to network but often with an imposed, top-down agenda - an approach Andy Hargreaves described as 'contrived collegiality'.

The effect of these 'ways' upon our own school's interaction with the community is admirably summed up by Pat and Colin Crane in their article 'Bosworth and the Community' in Chapter 3. They describe how Bosworth started as a Community College during the first way, became a Specialist Sports College during the second and third way, and has now re-engaged with the community as a fourth way Academy.

Hargreaves and Shirley saw the strengths and weaknesses of each of these periods and proposed a 'fourth way' that captured the best of the past, jettisoned the worst, and adopted new principles to meet the modern era. This philosophy was itself endorsed by Anthony Giddens (the intellectual architect of the 'Third Way'):

"In some places, Third Way politics have barely begun. In others, they have been pushed as far as they can go. It is high time for a new Fourth Way of social and

educational reform. In their unique and excellent text, Hargreaves and Shirley outline this way for the first time and provide crystal clear examples of what it looks like in practice."

We took the following nine principles from 'The Fourth Way' and aimed to embed them fully in our school. Ten years on, we feel confident that we have achieved this aim. As you can see, they are a combination of ideas from both the modern generation and previous eras:

1. Have an inspiring vision
2. Localise your learning
3. Be community-focussed
4. Forge ethical partnerships
5. Link with business and employers
6. Truly personalise your learning
7. Listen to, and act upon, the student voice
8. Assess intelligently
9. Develop your Professional Capital

These ideas led to a multitude of different projects which are too numerous to describe in detail here. Instead, we have devoted a chapter each to a few stand-out initiatives inspired by these principles and asked the people who led on them to describe their experiences. In Chapter 10, we outline an exciting development that blends all of these approaches together and in Chapter 11 we describe what Ofsted made of it all.

When we embarked on this journey there was little appetite for holistic education in England. Most schools were in PIXL and desperately trying to raise their outcomes, out-compete their neighbours, and avoid a visit from Ofsted. As such, many people questioned whether our fourth way initiative wasn't a distraction from our core purpose of churning out exam grades.

It wasn't until Ofsted themselves started to attack the exam factory system that some people became more receptive to our approach. The real turning point came in 2017 with Amanda Spielman's speech 'The Substance of Education'. In it she bemoaned the narrowing of the curriculum in many of the schools she had visited:

I have seen GCSE assessment objectives tracking back into Year 7, and SAT practice papers starting in Year 4. And I've seen lessons where everything is about the exam and where teaching the mark schemes has a bigger place than teaching history.

She didn't pull her punches about this approach to education:

This all reflects a tendency to mistake badges and stickers for learning itself. And it is putting the interests of schools ahead of the interests of the children in them. We should be ashamed that we have let such behaviour persist for so long.

It was refreshing to hear the head of Ofsted talk in this way (and admit Ofsted's own culpability in helping to create this situation in the first place), and it encouraged us to redouble our efforts. Having Ofsted apparently on our side for once was strange, but very welcome.

We wrote this book to celebrate all of the work that our colleagues and students have done and to provide ideas and inspiration for other people who work with young people - be they teachers, support staff, parents, or community and school leaders. It has been a collective effort, with every member of our staff having access to the draft manuscript.

This is, first and foremost, a practical book detailing Bosworth Academy's application of fourth-way ideas. Each chapter begins with a brief elaboration on the principle being discussed followed by relevant case studies. There is no particular order, so you can dip in and out as you wish. You might want to start with chapter one though, as the rest of the principles should reinforce the school vision. If you find the ideas interesting and want to know more, you should, of course, read 'The Fourth Way' itself.

Our fourth-way journey has been an exciting one and we hope you find reading about it as absorbing as we have found being on it.

Contents

"We've come to mistake curricular, textbooks, standards, objectives, and tests as ends in themselves, rather than a means to an end. Where are these standards and objectives taking us? What is the vision they are pointing towards? What purpose do they serve? What ideals guide us? Without ideals we have nothing to aim for. Unlike standards, ideals cannot be tested. But they can do something that standards cannot, they can motivate, inspire and direct our work."

Ron Richart

Chapter 1: Have an inspiring vision - Student Agency

Neely Gale - Post 16 student
Emmer Cooksey - ADT teacher

The first principle of The Fourth Way is to have an inspiring vision that motivates your staff and community. Ideally, this should be based on your traditional strengths and successes. With this in mind it seemed logical to make our vision 'A Learning Community' as Bosworth was one of the pioneering Leicestershire Community Colleges that Professor Hargreaves and Shirley described in 'The Fourth Way' in the following terms:

'At that time, innovative comprehensive schools such as the community colleges of Leicestershire...were open all hours to students and community members; they integrated educational services for young people with library, leisure, family, childcare and continuing educational services for adults; and they focused key parts of the project-based curriculum on community concerns.'

Our glass-dominated building was designed to illuminate the area at night and attract the whole community to use our facilities. As the first head, Tim Rogers, put it in his book 'School for the Community' (2):

'Why let half a million pounds' worth of building stand idle for all but seven hours a day, two hundred days a year?'

Our vision was to bring all of our educational stakeholders together to enrich our provision - whilst strengthening this community at the same time.

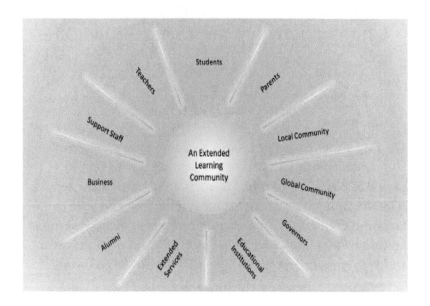

This community vision was effective and inspired a lot of the great initiatives we discuss in later chapters, but we always wondered whether it focussed on the students enough. And so, after learning about the OECD 2030 Learning Framework at a Whole Education Network conference, we decided to change our whole-school vision to the development of high-level student agency instead.

Agency is the underlying concept in the OECD model and it exactly matched our own educational philosophy. Agency is a mysterious term and in some countries there is no specific word for it. This is actually a positive because you don't want a whole-school objective to be too narrow or restrictive. For us it means empowerment, initiative and taking control over your own learning and life - particularly through the creation of crafted and beautiful work.

We called this pedagogical approach '3D learning' - make the learning deep, demanding, and developed, and we encouraged

A student with agency is...

Respectful of human dignity and the planet

Empowered

Self-directed

Defined by their integrity and values

Highly skilled and deeply knowledgeable

Prepared to stand up for their beliefs

An engaged citizen

A complex problem-solver

Mentally and physically well

A critical thinker and vocal questioner

A creative change-agent

A confident character

Multi-literate

An effective collaborator and communicator

A life-long learner

Future-ready

Bosworth Academy

active learning as students can't develop agency just by sitting and listening to the teacher. This led to numerous initiatives such as the project-based learning room, the film studio, the recording studio, the map room, the ADT student Instagram page, and our student-produced magazine - 'Zine'.

The Project-Based Learning Room

Student magazine -
'Zine'

***The initiative we particularly wanted to showcase in this chapter
was pioneered by Emmer Cooksey. However, we will start with
some thoughts from one of our students - Neely Gale:***

Case Study 1: A student perspective on agency
Neely Gale

Throughout my time at Bosworth the school has helped me develop agency both through my studies and the extracurricular activities and events that I have had the pleasure to be involved in.

At Bosworth, I have been involved in three whole-school strategic planning days and have helped collect the information to deliver for a fourth. These days have provided me with many unique opportunities to offer my views on the school and the learning involved. I also got an insight into the multiple methods and ways that teachers try to make our learning the best it can be.

During these days I was part of the student voice section of the day. Here a group of students would relay back to senior leaders responses to questions we formulated to discover students' feelings about the school. This includes lots of data collection before the actual day, which has helped me develop my public speaking, confidence, and teamwork skills.

The strategic planning day in 2019 also allowed me the opportunity to meet Olympic gold medallist Rebecca Adlington as she shared her educational story and how it led her to where she is today. It was an inspiring moment for me and many others in the room.

Bosworth has always supported the personal fundraising that I have carried out using many skills that Bosworth has taught me; so when the opportunity came up to help with the Ukrainian rehoming efforts and fundraising I was eager to get involved. In June and July of 2022, I set up a raffle that was done over the Bosworth Productions Show and Desford Heritage festival. To do this, we contacted many local businesses including Leicester Riders basketball, Triumph, Asda, Tesco, and the Co-op. I was supported by the school throughout the process and it helped me build many skills along the way.

In April of 2022, we filled out an application to become a refugee-friendly school through Citizens UK. We completed an awareness plan, action plan, and welcome plan that highlighted many things that the school would do to help welcome and provide wrap-around care for any refugee students that joined us.

We were awarded this accreditation in June when we attended an award ceremony at St James' The Greater Church in Leicester. We had to do a 3-minute speech to the rest of the successful applicants and the press explaining why Bosworth would make a fantastic place to welcome refugees. This helped develop my agency once again

I have also delivered numerous assemblies to multiple-year groups, ranging from subjects like mental health, our 'World-Class school' accreditation, how to act around Ukrainian guests, and many more. All of these assemblies built our Bosworth 6 C's and agency skills. I enjoy getting positive messages out to students and believe that student-led assemblies are great ways to develop agency.

When joining Year 12 I got involved with mental health wellbeing. This is where we were assigned a student from a younger year group who would talk to us about their time at school, how they are feeling, and what is occupying their mind. We then offered them advice, and talked to their teachers if needed.

World-class schools

I was also one of the six students who gained Bosworth the World-Class schools' accreditation. We went through a number of challenges, the first included us interviewing students and teachers in the first round to see if we would progress to the next stage. The second challenge was a day in Coventry at Riverbank Academy, a school for people with special educational needs.

As part of the day, we had to work with another academy as well as a primary school. As a group, we were tasked with revamping the Post-16 hub area of the school  adding a welcome sign, school rules, and a new planter by the entranceway. We each took on individual roles, my own being designer and resource coordinator. The day also included delivering a presentation on how successful our prior plans were, the benefit of what we have added to the school, and how well we worked in a group dynamic. The presentation was done in front of all the other schools and the head teacher of Riverbank. We gained personal reports from this day that evaluated us as students as well as how we worked together as a team.

After this day we were invited to the awards ceremony in London where we accepted the World Class School award and met up with some of our team members from task 2 again! From this, I have joined the World Class alumni which has allowed me to attend symposiums and later award ceremonies.

Case Study 2: The Lockdown Gallery
Emmer Cooksey - ADT teacher

Our students create beautiful work, that is no secret (or so we thought!). Traditionally in schools, we display student work around our classroom, showing off proudly what our students have done; artwork in the art classroom, MFL work in the MFL block, science diagrams in the science rooms, etc. If a student has created a beautiful piece of work and it is stuck on a wall in one classroom, usually only the teachers of that faculty and students being taught in the room would see it - that's great... But we started to ask ourselves: is it enough?

It occurred to us over the course of the pandemic, when we were torn away from most of our students, that their work needed recognition, in a BIG way. We were determined, however, to keep to our 3D philosophy and not just follow a knowledge-rich curriculum during lockdown. We decided to create our "beautiful work gallery" to do just that! By creating the gallery both online and within the school, it has allowed students of all abilities, especially those who perhaps felt like "underachievers" in terms of knowledge; to shine alongside their peers. Showing that beautiful work isn't just about knowledge and facts, but also the pride and effort you put into it. This has further fostered our culture of creativity and agency for the students - the more beautiful work submitted and displayed, the more we received, with students thrilled that they could show off their hard work for everyone at school and the community to see!

The work we were (and still are) seeing is deep, demanding, and developed; the students have taken ownership of their work, revealing them to be truly independent learners. Not only were they submitting work set by their teachers, but they were also producing work out of their own desire to create and continue learning - alongside the work set within the curriculum from all departments.

Additionally, the ADT Instagram page - (@bosworthacademyadt) set daily challenges for the students to explore their creativity within lockdown, resulting in some really great pieces of work that shed life on lockdown life.

Not being able to see their peers or our students, this small activity brought us together again - and created a feeling of a virtual community, even if we couldn't be in the classroom. This in turn helped our students' and staff's mental health. Although the challenges stopped once we were no longer all working from home, the gallery was such a success that we continued it in school after the students were allowed back, this fostered the incredible lift in student agency and engagement that still remains today.

With all departments having to come up with new ideas to keep our students engaged throughout home learning, we saw a rise in the setting of active and creative work as well as knowledge-based traditional learning. This allowed students of all key stages to produce work that they were not only proud of, but also helped their peers. For example, they produced A-level resources for other Business Studies students to share with each other, knowledge organisers for GCSE French and a revision resource for Blood Brothers. This nurtured the sense of community we have within school and allowed students to feel connected, especially throughout the pandemic.

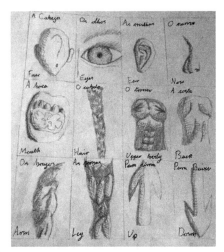

Alongside this type of work were also creative takes on home learning tasks, where students of all key stages had gone the extra mile with their work, showing off their art skills in English tasks for example. This hopefully helped cement the idea in the students' minds that each subject is connected, that their skills are transferable,

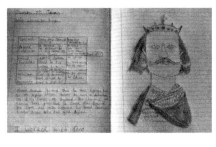

and that knowledge comes in many different forms.

Chapter 2: Localise your learning

Liam Grest - PE Team Leader

According to The Fourth Way, one drawback with the introduction of the National Curriculum in 1988 was that, by standardising the curriculum, schools could forget that they have a rich and unique locale that they can draw upon as inspiration for their teaching. To ensure that didn't happen at Bosworth, we created an 'Extended Learning Community' risk assessment policy which made taking students into the local community relatively easy for our staff. This led to such activities as helping to save the local library (by helping staff it with Post 16 volunteers for example), local village history walks, providing a home for Desford FC, and numerous other projects outlined in later chapters.

Working locally brings abstract concepts (such as the impact of the Norman Conquest) to life by making them concrete and real for the students. Indeed, our local learning provision has been written about in two books by Andy Hargreaves and Mick Waters:

'Others extend this community connection to the curriculum. For instance, Bosworth College—in the county of Leicestershire, where some of these colleges first started—fosters interdisciplinary inquiry into local issues such as the history of the English Civil War, including the major Battle of Bosworth Field, as well as the rise and fall of local coal mining.'
'Moving' by Andy Hargreaves, 2020 (3)

'Bosworth Academy in Leicestershire said of their approach to KS3: 'We see the local area as a valuable educational resource. We work with local employers and the community to enrich the learning experience for students whenever possible. This includes authentic projects like pre-apprenticeship programmes, saving the

local library, preserving nature reserves, mapping historic sites and connecting with local charities and the farming community'.
'About our Schools' by Tim Brighouse and Mick Waters, 2022 (4)

However, the initiatives we wanted to showcase in this chapter were led by Liam Grest - our head of PE and community leader at SLT, and three LSAs - Laura Spradbury, Amy Winterbottom, and Molly Sessions.

Case-study 1: Leicester Forest - cross-country history

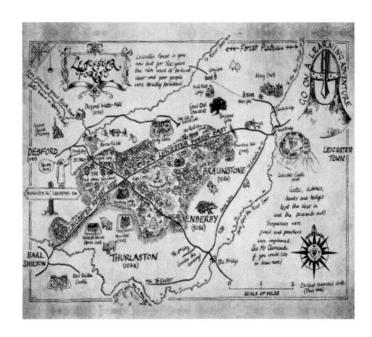

The Leicester Forest map above and a Year 7 student's lego version below

When the task of developing a unit of work based on our local area was set, the Physical Education team wanted to give our students the opportunity to physically visit the areas within our locale and immerse them in the topics studied in the classrooms.

From its inception, the Leicester Forest cross-country run has been an extremely popular aspect of our curriculum and has allowed us to explore the local countryside with our Year 7 students and teach them that the area in which they are standing was once a royal hunting forest.

The run that they complete is a 4km out and back run with the farthest point being at the top of the '29 steps', an ancient entrance to what was the Leicester Forest. When students arrive there, we explain the Norman privatisation of the forest for hunting; and their expulsion of the local Saxon villagers who were now unable to forage for food and had to trespass in order to survive.

During the second lesson of the week, we again run the students out to the 29 steps and then ask them to pair up. One partner adopts the role of a villager and the second takes on the role of a Forrester - the King's guards and game-keepers of the forest (see the photo of an ancient Forrester's lodge below). The role-play begins with the villager having a head start and running back towards the school with the Forrester in pursuit. If the villager arrives first then their family is fed. Should the Forrester catch the villager then they would be fined, or imprisoned.

This crime and punishment scenario really brings the learning to life through them imagining facing the dilemma of abiding by an unjust law or feeding their family. We also explore the notion of how local knowledge of the area allowed for a quick escape in the days before GPS and Google Maps - and ask them to consider what key points of the local geography they might use to guide

themselves? How, if you are arrested and taken to court and subsequently jailed, will your family survive?

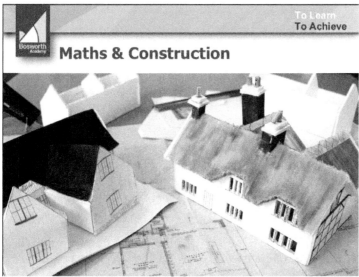

It proved a successful unit of work as the physical role-playing allowed students to immerse themselves in the local area and experience the emotions of peasants 1000 years prior.

Cross-Curricular, Project-based Learning

Year	Project Title	Big Question	Week 1	Week 2	Week 3	Exhibition
7	Leicester Forest	What was life like in Leicester Forest?	✓	✓	✓	✓
8	Environmental Awareness	How can we work together to help save the planet?	✓	✓	✓	✓
9	The Cold War	What was the Cold War and its legacy?	✓	✓	✓	✓

Timings 2016-2017

Later on in Year 7, the students continue the unit of work on local history by partaking in the 'Hereswode Games'. The Hereswode, or 'Wood of the People', was the name given to Leicester Forest by Viking Settlers in the area and local people would take part in annual events to compete against each other. In our games, the students' complete activities like 'Spurning the Barre' (Tossing the Caber), Putting the Shot, and Tug of War.

This experience again brings to life the history of how people would have lived and come together in community-based festivals on annual holidays. We link this to the wider world by referencing the Wenlock Games which happened in Shropshire and helped inspire the creation of the modern Olympic Games.

Fourth Way
Curriculum Development
To Learn
To Achieve

Bosworth Open Day, June 2016

A further unit of work focusing on our local area and Leicester Forest is the Year 8 Environmental activity where all students in Year 8 go on a 13km walk to Thornton Reservoir. The students are taken off the timetable for the whole day and walk, in groups of 20, from the school to the reservoir and back.

During the walk, the students experience public roads, public footpaths and rights of way, the local watermill, and an area of local natural beauty in the reservoir and its surroundings as well as encountering livestock in fields. The day really gives students an appreciation of local nature as well as challenging them physically to complete a strenuous 13km walk. It is clear that many of the students are not literate in terms of the countryside that surrounds the school - a memorable moment was when students were marvelling at this 'thing' on the floor; it was a cow pat. It was astonishing that they had never seen one before, and demonstrated how little some of our students interact with nature.

We also introduced orienteering lessons to utilise the full space of our school grounds. Students were given a map and a variety of control points that they had to locate and navigate to in the shortest time possible. Students became genuinely competitive during the activity and didn't realise that they were developing critical thinking and collaborative skills, as well as doing a great deal of exercise, because they were having so much fun.

Case-study 2: Henrichment

Molly Sessions, Laura Spradbury, and Amy Winterbottom (LSAs)

This project was run by two LSAs for a Year 7 support group. Laura and Amy no longer work at the school - but here is an article from the Leicester Mercury in 2016 about the project:

A school enrichment project is helping a group of students at one Leicestershire school to broaden their horizons.

Youngsters at Bosworth Academy have been able to swap the classroom for the great outdoors two hours a week.

Instead of whiteboards and textbooks, they have enjoyed farm and park trips among others.

The opportunity is aimed at boosting their confidence, opening up new opportunities, and taking advantage of the school's rural surroundings.

Learning mentor Laura Spradbury says: "It's having a massive impact on the 16 students taking part. We have 20 acres of grounds and are surrounded by countryside so we thought we should make the most of it. We wanted to take the pupils out of their ordinary environment and we all know the benefits that the great outdoors can bring.

"We're definitely seeing a change in the students involved. They've opened up more, they're communicating better, and they're not afraid to speak up in front of others, which is having a massive knock-on effect on the rest of their education elsewhere in the school."

46

Pupils have visited local parks, farms, falconry centres, and even restaurants where they have seen for themselves how food goes from farm to plate.

One of the highlights of their work has been building their own chicken coop and incubating some chicks which have since hatched.

"We've dubbed this our 'henrichment project'," says Ms. Spradbury.
"They've absolutely loved all the different elements of it and the chickens, now called Apollo and Delia, are just one part of it. Students have written about their experiences, got hands-on building and creating things, and are learning all about teamwork. It's given us a chance to teach them about healthy eating, they've enhanced their literacy skills by writing about their experiences, and we have also incorporated science and geography into it by learning about ecosystems and how communities live off one another. The opportunities really are endless and it's something we hope to push out to other students across the school."

Learning mentor Amy Winterbottom, added: "It really is fantastic to see the pupils blossoming in this way and so enthused about what they're doing. It just makes us want to strive even harder to give them the opportunities they deserve.

The Whole Education Network peer review 2016:
The "Henrichment" project has clearly had an impact on many students. Examples offered by the staff included much-improved attendance, an increase in the confidence of many students, and some students now engaging with the school to such a degree that an elective mute student had started to communicate.
Staff spoke of the impact of their work with joy and immense pride. The staff articulated how they had made connections for young people with how they live but also through the introduction of many real-world community engagements for the youngsters as part of the project including visits to and from farmers, restaurants, and a local market.

The pupil who helped to conduct the reviewer's tour was full of praise for the impact of the project on his peers and him. He was also very quick to talk about aspects of the academy's work, for example, the greenhouse growing project and the sports leaders' program.

With a little encouragement, support staff began to discuss how they could extend this project having evaluated its previous success. Their ambition and desire to be agents of change were great to see.

Whole education review 2018:
The "Henrichment" project clearly continues to have an impact on many students. The tremendous utilisation of space and trust shown in young people (also seen in the ponds and planting of the "new forest") all demonstrate how a curriculum that values the environment and young people creates a virtuous circle that leads to a richer school.

Since Amy and Laura left:

Over the years Henrichment has evolved into a living model which identifies some of our most vulnerable students and provides them with a safe space to blossom, learn, and safely practice self-expression and an appreciation of the different needs of other peers. Through using and adapting pre-existing ideas and developing new strategies and expectations, the children in these groups have now gained a great deal of security. The work undertaken by the students in the class not only requires them to conduct research and learn about the topics but it also provides them with the opportunity to work creatively and collaboratively. This gives them a sense of achievement and pride in their own abilities.

Molly Sessions (LSA)

Challenge Partners review 2022

"Henrichment is expertly run for a group of vulnerable YR7 students. These students are well supported in this group to engage and make progress. The students voiced that they enjoy the creative approach to their learning in a safe learning environment"

Chapter 3: Be Community-Focussed

Jane Alexander - Cultural Studies Team Leader
Sebastien Mainard - Modern Foreign Languages Team Leader
Abi Masih - English teacher and Literacy Coordinator
Adam Hodges, Communications Officer at Bosworth Academy

Schools have become a little like prisons in modern times. Fences now surround the perimeters, the inmates are not allowed out and visitors are closely monitored. This has led to schools being cut off from the very communities they are meant to serve. Educationally speaking this is particularly damaging because it makes education seem inauthentic to students who often struggle to see the point of what they are learning.

In their book 'The Unfinished Revolution', (5) John Abbot and Terry Ryan argue that, in many ways, the most authentic educational system was the old apprenticeship model where young people would learn their trade from an experienced master craftsman in the local community. They were immediately able to see the purpose of their work and how much it was valued by society. As a result, they were far more motivated to apply themselves and become lifelong learners. Obviously, we can't reinstate this system in the modern world - although Careers Weeks can simulate it to a degree. What we can do, however, is reach out and look for opportunities to reconnect with our communities wherever possible.

We interpreted community in its broadest sense and looked to strengthen our school community, and our local, national, and global communities as well. The American philosopher and educator John Dewey encouraged schools to think of themselves as microcosms of society and to develop little citizens rather than test dummies. We feel we should try to simulate utopia in schools and build our idea of a perfect society where kindness, decency, participation and life-long learning abound. Thinking about school communities in this way can be really thought-provoking and rewarding for everyone involved.

Reconnecting with our local community was something of a magical mystery tour. We went out trying to save the local library but ended up working with people and organisations we had not previously been aware of. The key person turned out to be Pat Crane, who seemed to be at the centre of all the good things going on in our village. It was through her that we made links with Caterpillar, the Barns Charity fields, local historians and community organisers.

Many of the resulting projects are outlined in other chapters and, for the past year, we have had a designated community coordinator role within SLT which has led to great work supporting local groups (especially during lockdown), and more recently, refugees from Ukraine. However, the initiatives we are showcasing in this chapter were led by our head of Cultural Studies, Jane Alexander, and Sebastian Maynard - our head of MFL. Firstly, though, we hear from Pat herself:

Reflections on the impact of the Fourth Way
by local community leaders - Pat and Colin Crane

Bosworth Academy in the Community

We have lived in Desford for over 50 years so have witnessed Bosworth Academy almost from its arrival in the village, as Bosworth Community College. I have been a member of the Parish Council for about 25 years and Colin for a shorter period. We have been involved with many community groups during this time. Memories of the early days include the many evening (and daytime) classes offered to the community, the youth club, and the Endeavour Club for those with disabilities.

Times changed and education provision with it. With the demise of the Community College, the school became cut off from the community (apart from the ongoing use of the swimming pool and other sporting facilities). It was physically on the edge of the village and people had no reason to visit unless they had children studying there.

Thankfully, that changed again and the school's relationship with the village has greatly improved. Much of the change has been due to the decision to adopt the principles of the Fourth Way and put them into practice as part of the student's everyday experience, not just as an add-on.

The school has, of course, expanded its age range and has once again become engaged with the community, albeit in a different way. This was always going to be a challenge, as the majority of the students do not live in Desford.

One of the earliest steps to renew the links with the community through the Fourth Way was in 2014 when the Academy worked with a group of residents to submit an expression of interest in keeping the library open - after the County Council made the decision to close many branch libraries.

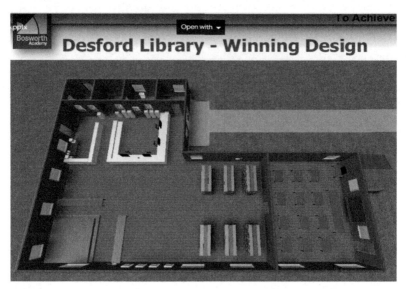

This resulted in the library becoming a Community Managed Library, run by volunteers. Over the years since then, a number of Bosworth students have volunteered at the library, often whilst working towards their Duke of Edinburgh award. We have also been pleased to see displays of students' artwork in the library.

The next milestone was an outcome of the discovery of the King in the Car Park. As we were on the route of Richard III's cortege in 2015, the White Rose initiative offered members of the community the opportunity to visit the school for workshops to make a rose. The resulting display of residents and students working outside the school was spectacular.

Also in 2015, the Elephant Garden was opened to the public as part of Desford Open Gardens weekend. Students had worked hard in their lunch hours to grow flowers and vegetables and to upcycle discarded filing cabinets. Sadly, the garden club was discontinued but, as we write, there is a plan to revive it under the guidance of another member of staff. We appreciate that it is not easy to facilitate out-of-hours activities.

Another link with the community has been through the choir singing in St Martin's Church. We would like to see this happening again.
For several years, senior citizens have been invited to the school near Christmas to be entertained with music, singing, and dancing performed by the students; whilst other students baked cakes and savouries and served refreshments. Any opportunity for intergenerational dialogue is always welcome. This was replicated this year with a Jubilee Tea for older members of the community.

As part of the Fourth Way, teachers have made more use of village facilities. Students began to use the Barns Charity fields and the brook which runs through them, for scientific and geographical studies.

The history of the village and its position on the fringe of Leicester Forest has also been incorporated into the students' studies, involving walks and runs around the Conservation Area and out as far as the forest boundary.

A good relationship has been built up with the Design Department and a group of students has participated in the annual Sewathon, organised by the Desford branch of Loving Hands. This involves bringing their sewing machines to the Church Centre and spending the day making children's clothes which are sent to developing countries. It inspired the 'Sew off to Africa' project in 2015/16. Paused by COVID, we hope that the Sewathon will start again next year.

The last academic year saw a leap forward with the appointment of a member of staff to lead on community liaison. Some of the younger students decorated a tree as part of the Christmas Tree Festival. Other students have done litter picks. Some have entertained the residents who attend the local dementia group.

Desford Heritage Festival was held this July, organised by a group of residents, and one student designed and produced 20

shields to represent the Duchy of Lancaster, which were displayed along the school fence. The Academy kindly allowed the school field to be used by one of the re-enactment groups plus a funfair, and the car park was available for the numerous visitors. (The car park has also been used for Desford Scarecrow Festival over the August Bank Holiday since 2017, though we have not seen an Academy scarecrow yet!).

The most recent project is again with the Design Department. A group of students has been asked to design and produce a series of mosaics which will be installed on the outside wall of Desford Library Community Hub.

We hope that all of the above-mentioned activities help to broaden the education of the

young people who pass through Bosworth Academy. Community engagement is a two-way process and, in our view, some of the initiatives which have emerged from the Fourth Way have proved to be very successful. Activities outside the classroom bring learning to life. We look forward to working together on further projects in the future.

Pat and Colin Crane

Case study 1: Our (Elephant) Community Garden

The philosophy of the Elephant Garden was to teach our students about the science of plant and pond life, food production, and healthy eating but we also wanted our garden to be a sanctuary for

wildlife and a beautiful, peaceful place that can be used by students, staff and everyone in the community.

Concerns around climate change were at the forefront of our ethos and we were trying to change the 'throw away' attitude many people have today and believe that most everyday objects can be upcycled to fulfil a new purpose.

We used many old bits and pieces from around the school  including filing cabinets, old tins, sinks, ladders, pallets, and bins. By using our leftover paint and crafting skills, we

 transformed them into planters and features for our garden.

The entire garden cost less than £100 to create and most of this was start-up costs of seeds and many, many bags of compost! We created compost bins to recycle all our food waste and paper and we used our greenhouse to grow lots of plants for our garden and to sell to provide us with enough money to buy seeds for next year.

The greenhouse, which had been unused for many years, was brought back to life by enrichment classes and tutor groups who cleaned and organised the space. It has also been a sanctuary for students who sometimes found the classroom environment difficult and found fulfilment in sowing seeds and nurturing them to grow. It was a learning space where conversations around plant propagation came to life and students could see first-hand why pollinators were necessary to turn a courgette flower into a courgette and how seeds could be harvested at the end of the flowering season to use again the following year.

We managed to use some of our produce to cook with and in an after-school club with Claire Brockhouse, created our own pasta sauce from the tomatoes and seasoned it with our home-grown herbs. We also used the brambles around the school fields to make our own blackberry jam.

The sculpture in the centre of our garden was commissioned by the late Tim Rogers, the first principal of this school, in memory of his son who tragically died young. Legend says it casts a shadow of an elephant when seen from a certain angle at a particular time of day. Only a few have seen it! Our garden design reflects this theme and our elephant can be seen from the viewpoint above.

Jane Alexander (Head of Cultural Studies)

On behalf of Desford Community Action Group, I would like to record our thanks to Jane Alexander for her sterling work on the Elephant Garden. We have written to Jane but felt that she should be commended to Senior Management and Governors for the many hours, above and beyond the call of duty, that she has spent working on the garden and involving the students. We were delighted that the Academy took part in the Open Gardens weekend for the first time - and hope that this will be repeated in 2017.

We hope that you think it was of benefit to the Academy to be involved.

Many thanks,

Pat Crane

The Elephant garden is being revitalised from the academic year 2022-23 to bring it back to its former glory. The plan is to turn it into a memorial garden, in keeping with the sad reason for the sculpture's installation in memory of the son of Tim Rodgers, the first Bosworth College Headteacher.

The project will recreate the outline of the elephant's ear as a flower bed with collaboration between staff members and students who will help plant and maintain the garden throughout the year. We also aim to link with the 'Desford in Bloom' group to make stronger links with the local community.

Liam Grest

Case study 2: Our French Exchange

The French Exchange with Collège Jean Delacour in Rouen has been a great success and has enabled us to expand our learning community enormously. Each year around 30 Year 8 students spend a week in and around the school or their students come to us. This enables students to socialise and practise their French with their peers in an authentic environment.

Students work on projects which emphasise our shared experiences - such as our Norman past. The French students' visit to our school remains one of the highlights of the year and it is lovely to see students interacting with each other informally and breaking down linguistic and cultural barriers - especially in the age of Brexit!

Whole education peer review 2016:

In terms of the stated intention of engaging with the local community, governors, business, support staff, and teachers, the Fourth Way projects were clearly working. The recent introduction of a French partner school has been used to make connections across the curriculum in terms of local history and the common Norman heritage, PE, drama, and the community garden.

Students have had extensive interactions with their French counterparts, including visits, exchanging Christmas cards, 'Skyping' their school, and joining a Norman tour of Rouen. This has started to develop a global dimension where real-life friendships have increased the relevance of the curriculum and need to be embedded as part of a long-term plan used to make connections across the curriculum.

French Trip Success - In the Loop newsletter
Students from Years 8, 9, and 10 thoroughly enjoyed their visit to France between Monday 20 June and Friday 24 June. Students showed great character when our departure from school was delayed and we were blessed with lovely weather during our trip.

We visited Sword Beach in Normandy and contemplated the sacrifices soldiers made during World War II before showing great Citizenship skills by working with students at the Collège Jean Delacour near Rouen. Students were able to visit the city of Rouen and enjoy the sights and sounds before we returned back to England. Well done to all students!
Mr. Mainard, Curriculum Leader MFL.

Case study 3 - The power of peers - the student community

At the start of the 2020 academic year, the SLT at Bosworth Academy was concerned about the lack of engagement among the Year 10 Pupil Premium (PP) students with online learning during the first lockdown. Those concerns were supported by **qualitative data** (feedback from teachers, Head of Faculty, and Head of Year 10) but also by **quantitative data** based on the list of students who had not engaged in remote learning, as well as the quantity of work sent back on our homework software called "Show-my-homework".

This was also a national concern, as Sam Butters and Gina Cicerone, co-chief executives of the Fair Education Alliance and partners on the report, said: *"Before Covid-19, persistently disadvantaged children were already **22 months behind** their more advantaged peers, and it is widely expected this will increase as a result of school closures."* (Children & Young People Now- 26/08/2020.)

Therefore, I decided that my project would contribute to bridging the learning gap between our Year 11 PP students and the other Year 11 students for the academic year 2020-2021. However, after the second lockdown, I carried on my project with the next cohort of Year 11 for the academic year 2021-2022. It was agreed with SLT that I will focus on English, Maths, and Science.

Firstly, I concentrated on identifying a national picture of the PP students' attainment. Before the pandemic, in the article published by the Education Endowment Foundation (EEF) in 2017 called "the Attainment Gap", it says that "the widest attainment gap is for the disadvantaged students who are FSM and SEN". The Average Attainment 8 score for all other pupils is 51.6 whereas for FSM it is 39.0. This represents a difference of 12.6.

Secondly, to narrow my research in identifying the needs of the PP students, I used SISRA. However, I was not able to have a reliable source of DATA information until the first trial exams which took place in December 2021. I used the trial exam results as a reference for my DATA analysis and compared it with the previous cohort's trial exam in 2019-20.

The average total attainment 8 for PP students for the trial exam in December 2021 was 27.70 whereas for non-PP it was 31.89, which equals an attainment gap of 4.19. The average progress 8 for PP was -1.41 whereas the average progress 8 for non-PP was: -1.11. If I compare this cohort with the previous one, the attainment gap for last year's cohort's trials was surprisingly worse: 7.37. However, the average Progress 8 variations between PP and non-PP remained very similar: 0.30 for the cohort of 2020/21 and 0.29 for the cohort of 2019/20.

Therefore, after the trial exams, it became clear that there was still a gap between the PP students and the non-PP students even if it appeared smaller than last year. However, the difference between the PP and non-PP in making progress remained the same.

I used Kotter's eight steps process theory to show how I introduced my new project. Steps 1, 2, and 3 are about creating the climate for change. Thus, I first ensured that my project responded to a new need of the school. I consulted with SLT and ELT to make sure that my project complemented any other initiatives which already existed in the school and that it brought something new. I created what Kotter calls a sense of urgency, which means showing staff what the point of the change is all about.

Then, I did what Kotter explained in step 2, which was to build the team by involving the Heads and Lead Practitioners of English, Science, and Maths faculties to participate in the training of the peer mentors. I also involved the Heads of Faculties by asking them to provide relevant revision material for the students.

The third step is about creating the vision and for that I undertook extensive research into peer mentoring and what it can bring to more vulnerable students. For example, using an article published by the EEF, I was able to share this citation during my presentation to ELT: *"Overall, the introduction of peer tutoring approaches appears to have a positive impact on learning [...] Though all types of pupils appear to benefit from peer tutoring, there is some evidence that **pupils who are low-attaining and those with special educational needs make the biggest gains**."* Furthermore, it is important to state that the EEF teaching and learning toolkit rates peer mentoring at +5 which is a significant score to convince colleagues about the importance and the impact of the project.

The second important part of the theory of Kotter is engaging and enabling the organisation to embrace change. During our ELT meeting in October 2021, I presented the peer mentor project's aims and vision: what it involves; what I needed from my middle leader colleagues; how it was going to take place, and why it was an important project for our PP students. Then, I recruited and trained the peer mentors from Year 12. Following the empowering step (Kotter), I developed a peer mentor training programme so new mentors understood their role and responsibility in the project.

Finally, one of the most important stages of Kotter's theory is about implementing and sustaining change. After a fantastic start, we experienced a second lockdown. This was a challenge for the continuity of the project, but I managed, via our online setting, to enable peer mentoring sessions to continue. Half of the group stuck to the project and engaged regularly with their mentors online. When students came back to School in April, this group got back together and strengthened their collaboration. This created a new dynamic that attracted other students to join the project.

Therefore, due to its success, the project was carried on in September with more peer mentors and more Year 11 students. The project is still running and has proven to have a positive impact on all students. The peer mentoring scheme has become part of the culture and normal provision in our school. As Kotter describes in his last step, change needs to be accepted and sustained over time. He mentions that change needs to be sustainable to "make it stick" in an organisational culture. This project has been accepted and embraced by the school and by students.

Mentoring for achieving - newsletter article

The peer mentoring project has started again this year and it has been running for the last 4 weeks. But what is peer mentoring exactly? "Mentoring is a structured and trusting relationship between a young person and a caring individual who offers guidance, support, and encouragement" In this project, it is 20 Year 13 students who mentor 20 Year 11 students twice a week, for ½ hour during tutor time.

The sessions take place in the canteen around a hot chocolate. There is a fantastic and studious atmosphere, our Year 11 students enjoy working with their mentor and value the one-to-one support. It is an opportunity for them to learn and revise key topics and gain practice on exam questions. It is also a chance to learn from the experience of an older student who has been in the same situation not so long ago.

Trust is everything and the peer mentors use this to connect their students to learning. This project made a real difference for Year 11 last year. Students improved academically, they achieved better grades, and most of all they improved their attitude towards learning. Teachers noticed better participation in lessons and homework completion got more consistent.

Based on this success, the project has recruited 30 more Year 12 students this year who are being trained for their new role in our School community. Those students should start in 2 weeks' time and join the Year 13. This will make around 50 Year 11 students who get the extra support to achieve at GCSE and considerably improve their prospects for their future.

Mr. Mainard, Senior Leader

Reading Academy
Abi Masih - English teacher, and Literacy coordinator

Reading Academy was set up a few years back to support those with weak literacy skills. It is an opportunity to improve the reading skills of Year 7 and Year 8 students with the support of Post 16 students. The programme allows both Post 16 and Key Stage Three students to work together; providing the former with an enrichment opportunity  and the latter a reading intervention. Year 13 students Harry B, Reme O, and Jess P have been mentoring Key Stage Three students for two years where the younger students read aloud to the Sixth Formers before doing book quizzes. "It is really nice when the students do their book quizzes and pass," said Reme O. Harry B agreed and said the students get a great sense of "satisfaction and they feel that they have achieved". Reme O added that she "loved" helping the students pick out a book that interests them and said that students who "don't like reading have just not found the right book."

Literacy was praised by Ofsted in the recent report:

Reading is a priority in this school. Leaders have developed a programme to help all pupils become more confident readers. Leaders make sure that pupils who need help to improve their reading get the right support. Pupils read a wide variety of challenging texts in lessons. The school's library is an inviting place where books and reading are celebrated.

Strong Communications for Strong Public Engagement

By Adam Hodges, Communications Officer at Bosworth Academy

"Either write something worth reading or do something worth writing about." Benjamin Franklin

Today's pace of life makes it seem that the world is forever spinning faster and faster on its axis. For messages to be conveyed in this environment they should be relevant and meaningful to an audience so they can be heard through the wall of noise which is punctuated with the sound of mobile phone notifications.

The ability to communicate strongly is seen by employers as hugely desirable in the workforce following the COVID-19 pandemic. A 2020 survey of global corporate recruiters by the Graduate Management Admission Council (GMAC) identified that the top three growing demands are: Managing Strategy and Innovation; Managing Tools and Technology; and Interpersonal Skills.

It is therefore imperative that the execution of our vision and values will provide students with the platform to excel in jobs, industries, and careers that may not even exist at the time of writing.

We must lead by example and utilise methods of communication in the classroom and teach students how to use them in a responsible and effective manner.

At the heart of our values at Bosworth Academy are the Global Competencies, affectionately known as the '6Cs' - Character, Collaboration, Citizenship, Creativity, Critical Thinking, and Communication. These competencies are not mutually exclusive as a student's ability to think creatively and critically can inspire peers to do the same, allowing them to work collaboratively and develop student agency by building confidence through citizenship and character. The remaining competency of communication enables students to share ideas and refine their work with constructive feedback from staff and fellow students.
After I was introduced to Hargreaves and Shirley's *'The Fourth Way'* (2009) I was soon able to identify that the ethos at Bosworth Academy is of responsibility and sustainability with the aims being to inspire and innovate. Hargreaves and Shirley propose that the 'Fourth Way' of educational development is made up of "six pillars of purpose and partnership. These are:

- An inspiring and inclusive vision;
- Strong public engagement;
- Achievement through investment;
- Corporate educational responsibility;
- Students as partners in change;
- Mindful learning and teaching." (Hargreaves and Shirley, 2009: 73)

I am going to focus on 'Strong public engagement' and how my role looks to sustain this as well as exploring new opportunities to communicate the vision of Bosworth Academy being a 'Fourth Way' school in action.

The importance of schools having strong public engagement was seen by Orr and Rogers, in *Public Engagement for Public Education* (2011) as "education works best when students, parents, and community members are engaged in improving the school system." (2011: xiii)

I look back on my own childhood with the internet in its infancy in the 1990s when school emails, social media posts, and websites were just a mere glint in a web developer's eye. My parents and I would huddle around an FM radio listening to the local station to hear if my school had been added to the 'Snow Day - School Closure' list. School updates were printed out on to a blue-papered newsletter at the end of term and school productions were recorded on video camera, available some weeks later on VHS.

The advancement of technology and the demand for immediacy have meant that schools have had to grow their means and methods of communication to keep their stakeholders informed. The need to communicate vital information for students and their parents/carers was magnified during the COVID-19 pandemic as schools were forced to close their doors to students. This inability to have face-to-face teaching saw the emergence of virtual teaching using web-conferencing applications like Google Meet, the online sharing platform Google Classroom and on the wider Google Drive in the G-Suite of applications that schools such as Bosworth Academy are licensed with. This innovation allowed staff and students to adapt to home learning and retain knowledge. It was identified that maintaining communication with parents and other stakeholders was vital during the pandemic. As a result of this, it was decided to turn the termly newsletter into a weekly one where Bosworth Academy could keep everyone 'In the Loop' - the name stuck and we have been producing In the Loop newsletters every week during term time since then. The newsletter is in the form of a PDF document with interactive web links and is communicated via email to parents and carers, published on the school's website, and shared on the school's social media platforms.

The newsletter itself contains a Headteacher's Welcome which summarises the events of the week and includes any important notices. Newsletter articles vary but contain events that have occurred in school that week, important notices, staff contact details, book recommendations from the 'Compass' library and even the lunch menu for the following week!

Since taking up the position of Communications Officer in April 2022 I have looked to develop themes and special content to engage the reader - this has included an alumni section where I have been in contact with previous students and have featured them in articles. Special features written by current students have also been included, increasing their student agency and developing their creativity and collaboration competencies.
I am always looking to innovate and in the Summer 2022 term, I devised a Google Form survey to gauge readership views on the newsletter. From this feedback, I have implemented a hot linked Table of Contents to ease navigation and have kept the newsletter to the preferred length to keep the reader engaged.

Bosworth Academy is in the Leicestershire village of Desford and households and local businesses around the area receive free magazine publications with news stories and advertisements included. I have increased the school's engagement with the wider community by submitting newsletter stories, including ones written by students, to these publications and they have been published. As well as physical copies, these local magazines now offer a digital copy that can be read on their website. This coverage has also been supplemented by having stories of A Level and GCSE Results Days printed in the Leicester Mercury, the regional newspaper across Leicestershire, and on their website.

The overall trend now shows readers going online to get their news with 98% of all internet users in the UK visiting a social media platform every month (IPSOS, August 2021). It is therefore critical that Bosworth Academy has a visible social media presence with the school having Facebook, Instagram, Twitter, and YouTube accounts. These social media channels allow messages to be conveyed quickly and the content varies from video/photos of events to important notices like job vacancies. Furthermore, from April 2022, I added LinkedIn to Bosworth Academy's portfolio of social media platforms to strengthen relationships with previous students, current staff, and potentially new staff members.

Not all stories are shared across the platforms as I tailor the message for varying audiences and it is important to have a visible presence when reporting on events at the school. When I was at  university my lecturer, and former journalist, Jonathan Foster, told me to always go to where the story happens and I still hold that true today - taking my camera around the school to report the great work being done at Bosworth Academy. This has included me accompanying staff and students on school trips such as: the GCSE

Business visit to Cadbury's World in Birmingham; the GCSE Geography students doing fieldwork in the Peak District in Derbyshire; and the female Engineering students being given a tour of the nearby Caterpillar factory in Desford, Leicestershire, on Women in Engineering Day. By taking part in these trips I can fully understand what the students learn from them and can vividly report back to stakeholders and enhance public engagement.

Reporting on school events and conveying the message via social media has enabled strong communication for strong public engagement to happen.

Recently a school-wide event was organised by Year 13 student and Stage Four cancer survivor, Kiya K. The event saw each year group complete a Gold Ribbon Run where students did laps of the school field to raise money for the Children's Cancer and Leukaemia Group charity. Prior to the event, I posted on social media a video of Kiya promoting the charity run and also sent an email to parents and carers, reminding them to donate. Over £900 at the time of writing was raised by the students - a fabulous achievement and I tagged the cancer charity's Twitter handle @CCLG_UK when I tweeted about this accomplishment. This was acknowledged by CCLG who Quote Retweeted - thanking the students for their efforts and we are now proud to say that the Head of Fundraising at CCLG is following Bosworth Academy on

Twitter - a true example of the Fourth Way in action.

That is just a sample of the work we are doing in using strong communications for strong public engagement. We continue to explore new opportunities to spread the word about the possibilities available through Bosworth Academy. This includes organising school visits from previous students who are excelling in their chosen industries to inspire the next generation of Bosworth Academy students. We are also exploring different communication channels to attract the new intake of students who will benefit from the Fourth Way.

Strong communications from Bosworth Academy to respective stakeholders and the wider community are therefore vital in developing, sustaining, and growing public engagement. It is our responsibility to innovate inside and outside the classroom to motivate and challenge students to be better than they thought they could be.

Adam Hodges, 25/9/2022

The Fourth Way, Andy Hargreaves and Dennis Shirley, 2009, Corwin.
Public Engagement for Public Education, Marion Orr and John Rogers (Ed.), 2011, Stanford University Press.

Chapter 4: Forge ethical partnerships

Matt Blackmore - Head of Geography

As schools increasingly focussed on outcomes during the 'second way' of education they became ever more inward-looking and obsessed with results and league tables. The third way in England saw a concerted effort to encourage networking amongst schools to raise standards. This development was welcome but rather top-down in approach - with the agenda often rigidly proscribed from above. The fourth way encourages schools to set their own agendas based on their unique character and context and to reach out to organisations that will enrich the lives of their students.

We have connected with numerous outside organisations in the past 10 years (educational networks, charities, councils, etc.) and achieved a variety of awards and accreditations. For example, we have gained Arts Mark, Careers Mark, World Class School, and Historic England School status. We also achieved Investors in People (gold) and The Whole Education Network adjudged us to be 'Transformational'.

These networks have connected us to uplifting communities in a voluntary and bottom-up way and have enriched our educational provision immeasurably. The initiative we wanted to showcase here, however, was led by our Head of Geography - Matt Blackmore:

Case Study - Environmental Partnerships

We have been able to forge partnerships with numerous ethical organisations to enhance our students' understanding and awareness of environmental issues.

For example, with the support of funding from the **Woodland Trust**, the school grounds have been developed as a sustainability resource and we have actively planted a total of 300 new trees. We are also keen contributors to the **National Forest** endeavour. We have maintained a further 300 trees on the grounds and managed them as mature and semi-mature woodland.

The school has combined these physical and ecological developments with a cross-curricular programme that has enabled us to bid for both the **Eco-schools** award and a **Green Tree Schools** award. This has involved embedding, for the first time, an enrichment programme for Years Six and Seven which has become popularly known amongst students as "Tree Project!".

About 1/3 of all our Year 8 students have been learning "Forest School" skills and natural history. This has involved visits to **Leicester University Attenborough Arboretum**, health assessments of our own woodland stock, species identification, and biology and geography-related fieldwork on site. We plan to

expand this programme further to help students acquire woodcraft skills, experience visits from a tree surgeon, and capitalise on using the wild harvest from our new woodland in years to come.

We also link with the **Barns Fields Charity Trust** which enables

us to take students over the road to the historic fields which are a managed ecosystem and allow us to teach geography, history, poetry, and art in an authentic and inspiring context. This has led to some of the most memorable learning experiences our students have had at Bosworth.

Linking with environmentally-concerned **alumni** and **global experts** through Skype also connects the past and future very powerfully. For example, students were able to talk to an ex-student Vulcanologist in Montserrat as he sat beside his swimming pool - an advert for education if ever there was one! They also got to Skype a scientist whilst he was researching ice fields in Antarctica!

In an effort to showcase our green credentials we have conducted and recorded a multimedia "Virtual protest" filmed on the school field where all Year 8 students created banners to raise awareness on environmental issues - this involved a week of researching and publicising issues such as Food Waste, Acid Rain, Climate

Change, and Habitat Destruction. We also convened a student focus group that has gone from strength to strength known as the Eco-group - who have presented assemblies and worked toward peer education on environmental issues.

After a visit to the **Veolia** waste recycling plant in Mansfield, we negotiated a new recycling contract and ALL classrooms and communal areas now have a recycling bin for mixed materials. After a successful trial, these are now used daily and our school waste output has reduced significantly in terms of recyclables.

The combined efforts and projects listed above have been championed by staff, students, and governors alike; parents have been involved too. The school's recent Ofsted inspection rated us as an Outstanding school and recognised the significance of the many environmental projects and enrichment opportunities created from our efforts in gaining the grading we did.

I hope the material detailed above gives a comprehensive picture of how forging ethical partnerships can greatly enhance the quality of your provision.

Teaching about sustainability and being an **Eco-School** is about so much more than just the facts - these could be delivered very easily within a classroom, but by truly embedding these values across and beyond the curriculum we hope to engage, stimulate and create environmental ambassadors among our students and community for the future.

Chapter 5: Link with business and employers

Mike Winterton - Head of Engineering and Construction
Marie Delage-Martin - Head of Careers

It can be challenging to forge links with businesses because they are, well, very busy. Developing entrepreneurialism had been strongly encouraged during the 80s in England and Business Studies remains a popular choice - but actually taking students into work-places still remains relatively uncommon, and getting them to actually join is virtually unheard of. Nevertheless, it is well worth trying because, when it works, the experiences you can give the students are extremely powerful as they link to their aspirations and open their eyes to worlds they have never encountered before.

We managed to form valuable relationships with a number of local employers such as Next, Jaguar Landrover, and the Marriot Hotel. We also achieved Careers Mark 'Gold' in 2015 and 2022 and became Gatsby Benchmark compliant in 2021. However, the initiatives we wanted to showcase here were led by our Head of Engineering and Construction - Mike Winterton, and by our Head of Careers - Marie Delage-Martin.

Case study 1 - Caterpillar Pre- Apprenticeship Programme

In July 2015 we established a pre-apprenticeship programme with Caterpillar - which is the largest employer in our area. The stated aims of the course were to make our Year 12 intake engineers work-ready. To do this we designed a course structure that concentrated on the student, not the content. Desirable outcomes were self-confidence, drive, self-direction, and the ability to work independently and as part of a team.

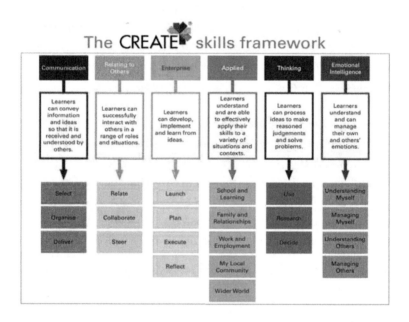

The CREATE skills framework seemed to fit the requirements but the question was how to make it work?

The Caterpillar pre-apprenticeship program was designed to provide students with aspirations and linked learning experiences in a real-life setting. Caterpillar was kind enough to allow regular access to their facilities and we were able to attend the site on a regular basis, gaining fantastic learning experiences that we would not have otherwise been able to access.

The program that we designed was in line with the principles of the Fourth Way - a holistic approach to education where students should be able to demonstrate the ability to work with others, take responsibility for their own learning, make the learning relevant for a modern age and build resilience and adaptability. Teach the students independence and tap into their passion for the subject and they will want to learn for themselves. Setting students a relevant and complex problem or project of this type is invaluable.

One of the problems that Caterpillar gave us was set by Birmingham Metropolitan College (Caterpillar's training partner at the time), to undertake a project for a local scout group in Broughton Astley. The project was the complete

renovation of a rickshaw.

Nicky Morgan, Secretary of State for Education opens Caterpillar's Learning & Inspiration Centre

It is worth remembering at this point that none of these students had had any experience with the tools or materials that they had to use to create a quality product at no cost.

We were tasked with renovating the rickshaw with a minimal budget and a short time frame. The students reused and recycled materials to achieve this result. The scout group supplied the original machine, a new battery, and a sound system, and the

89

students made everything work as it should, based on experiential learning or research.

When the rickshaw was complete we had a little handover and thank you session. This is very important to the process as it gives ownership and reinforcement of the positive experiences that the students have gained in an immediate way.

During this journey, Caterpillar was massively supportive with tours and visits. We were invited regularly to meet designers and engineers and received training sessions from industry experts.

We even got to have a whole day (7.30 am start 4 pm finish) on their virtual training platform - including the standard work system (S.W.E). Assembling products in a real-life environment, and using full-size equipment in real-time with immediate feedback was extremely powerful. This was a very important stage of the course with students maturing almost before our eyes. The teamwork and critical thinking that was evident on that day was probably the single most important event of the course.

The sheer scale of the event was huge - with hundreds of components, real work methods, the noise from the conveyor belts, smells from the machinery, echoes from the vast area of the training facility, and interactions with the five trainers to provide the next steps and feedback. Even the fact that the students took their breaks in the canteen with the rest of the employees all added

to the overall realism of the experience. Students went home tired but enthused.

The teamship this course built and the love of learning that this has germinated were evident in the extracurricular activities that the students organised. They took part in a Sunday run and 5km obstacle course through the muddy, wet countryside. They also built and entered a vehicle in a downhill racer competition.

The Whole Education Network peer review:

The Pre-apprentice programme in engineering demonstrated an excellent development of space. The teacher and the young people following the course had clearly grown as a result of its creation. The partnership work with Caterpillar and others has translated what may have been a disjointed experience into something transformative. It was particularly heartening that, having heard

Key Stage Three students articulate their experience in enrichment lessons and the Leicester Forest project, Key Stage Five students could see how their course was an extension of the same philosophy. They would clearly like the opportunity to start again and experience a six-year journey based on the same principles.

The future

The pre-apprenticeship programme became a victim of the school's academic success as high student outcomes led to less demand for a vocational pathway. However, we have maintained our links with Caterpillar and are relaunching our partnership through a STEAM project involving multiple departments. Watch this space!

Case Study 2 - Careers Education

Marie Delage-Martin - Head of Careers Education

My professional pathway led me to Careers Education about 15 years ago and I always found it so fascinating and a powerful tool for positive change for both staff and student aspirations.

When I started, like many schools, Bosworth had Connexions advisers and, although they did offer one-to-one interviews and some flyers and documents, the approach (despite the name) was very disconnected and operated outside the Bosworth experience rather than being a part of it. Careers were not really seen as a core priority by staff and more as an adjunct.

When the coalition government came into power, Connexions was disbanded and funding for Careers education was withdrawn. This presented us with a challenge but also an opportunity to rebuild and do something more impactful. At approximately the same time, the school got a new head-teacher and Bosworth started its very own journey called the Fourth Way.

Firstly, we decided to keep a budget for Careers and ended up employing our own Careers adviser. This enabled us to maintain a good provision for the transition of our students. We also used a new system to track the destination of our students. Before this, the process was very haphazard and we were not able to identify students who may need support or raising aspirations. This was our first step. We also got support from our local LLEP and Enterprise adviser.

The next step was to put ourselves through the rigorous process of an external assessment called Career Mark. The process was very constructive, enabled us to see our strengths and what needed to be developed and mostly it gave us access to our students' voice as a representative section of the students were interviewed as part of the process. The main advantage at the time was that we were able to discover and take account of the Gatsby benchmarks which are now so vital in any school's Careers provision. This was years before the DfE decided that all schools should be expected to meet all benchmarks in time.

Armed with a streamlined programme, students' voice and our firm belief in the benchmarks, we started to put in place interventions across the school. For example, we now have a major 'Meet the employers' event for each cohort with a different focus depending on the year group. Year 7 attend a 'Guess My Job' session with a variety of employers while Year 12 will have mock job interviews. We even managed to conduct these during the lockdown online which we were very proud of as many schools cancelled all such events. Various pathways are promoted including apprenticeships and T levels as well as university.

We also developed staff training in Careers education by offering bespoke programmes and having a Careers Champion in each Faculty. Each subject contributes to the delivery of Careers education so that it is not just seen as someone else's responsibility. We also have alumni coming to talk to our students about where their education has taken them.

SLT and ELT are fully committed to Careers education and have supported our programme and ideas effectively for many years now. The inception of the 6 Cs values across the school and the Real Life programme was also instrumental in raising the profile of Careers education and making the students and the staff see it as an essential part of our offer to young people and not as the adjunct it was all those years ago.

The best part of my teaching life is seeing the positive interactions the kids have with employers. Some students who are harder to reach often behave so well and engage with employers, especially when the encounter is planned well and involves interaction and not just passive listening (this is unfortunately not always possible and not every employer comes across well in front of an audience of young people so you need to choose your employer volunteers well).

It is also extremely rewarding when employers praise our young people and their approach. One of the highlights for me was when an employer said the experience had totally changed her perception of young people for the better. So these multiple encounters serve a dual purpose and enrich both students and employers alike. Every individual interaction or dialogue with a teacher or employer contributes to the web of Careers education in our school community. You have to think big and small too.

We have so much to do, develop and explore. Our next journey is a MAT-wide one, we have mirrored our own structure for Careers and work-related learning across our schools, with a similar staff and leadership structure to enable better collaboration (one of our 6 Cs in action) but also taking care to build an ethos where each school is allowed to be individual and embrace its own unique history and context. We want our young people to feel confident they can take their first steps in the world of work and realise that learning is for life

Chapter 6: Truly personalise your learning

Gemma Grant - Business and IT Team Leader
Esmee Boyall - Lead Practitioner
Becky Green, Brogan Penlington, Lisa Ravel - Performing Arts team

Truly personalising learning is about tapping into each individual student's interests, passions, and aspirations. This can seem very difficult but, in fact, when we interviewed our Year 7 students, we found that their interests tended to group around sport, performance, creativity, and technology - all of which could be catered for by a mindful curriculum and a vibrant co-curricular programme.

Mick Waters talks about seeing every lesson as just a cobble in the road of each and every student's life. Just as a single cobble is only of use as part of a whole, teachers should try to connect each lesson to everything else in the student's life (previous lessons, other subjects, home life, interests, future careers etc.), rather than just seeing it as a discrete unit of learning. This will build a deeper understanding of a subject, a greater awareness of the big picture, and also engender in the student a sense of purpose and destiny.

When we do truly personalise the learning the results can be astounding, as can be seen in the following case studies led by our Business and IT team leader - Gemma Grant, our Lead Practitioner Esmee Boyall, and our performing arts team - Becky Green, Brogan Penlington and Lisa Ravel.

Case study 1 - Extended Project Qualifications
Gemma Grant - Business Team Leader

Post 16 students have the option of picking EPQ (Extended Project Qualification) as one of their 4 A Levels. This option is completely different from traditional A Levels as it is entirely personalised to what each student wants to achieve. Students develop their own hypotheses and set out on their own journey to achieve the outcomes to prove it right or wrong.

Their EPQ journey takes them through the skills of research, referencing, analysing, questioning bias, evaluating, and finally synthesising the results. Students produce a 5000-word essay or an artefact accompanied by a research report. The topic of their project can be whatever they are passionate about or want to know more about. This might be based around a hobby, a potential future career, or an additional A Level topic that they couldn't pick, the list is endless.

Some examples of previous titles have been:

Why are buildings designed differently around the world?
How is virtual reality affecting the future?
What are the implications of childhood poverty on a child's education and why should we care?
Is sustainable growth actually achievable?
Is claiming insanity a loophole for criminals?

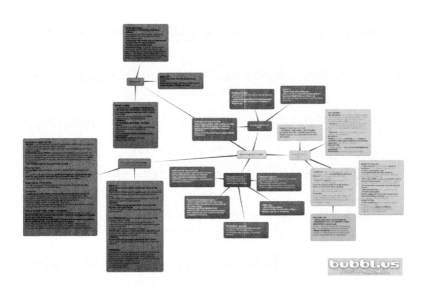

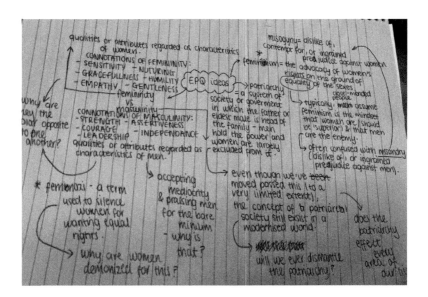

Teaching takes a very different approach in this course, which
students take a while to adjust to. The teacher is not telling them

what to do and what to complete, the ideas and passion have to come from the students themselves. Once they have an idea the student's supervisor will meet with them regularly to discuss how they are getting on. The supervisor will not give them answers, but poses questions to make the student question, analyse and articulate their research up to that point.

How has the EPQ benefited me as a student?

-The EPQ has allowed for me to develop my research skills especially using qualitative and quantitative sources to back up my points. It has also allowed for my to develop my synthesis skills when using sources to backup my points and ideas even if the source is outdated.

-The EPQ has also taught me how to effectively develop ideas and how to reference sources and back up my ideas and points effectively. These skills are useful as I can transfer them to my other subjects and use them at university.

-Skills that could be improved were my lack of primary data such as questionnaires and interviews to back up my essay rather than rely on secondary sources.

In essence, the students are completing a mini dissertation. They complete the essay alongside a literature review and a full plan as to how they got to the end results. Once the essay is complete students have to complete a 10-minute presentation to a number of staff, explaining their findings and also how the journey they have been on has impacted them. Universities love students who have completed an EPQ because it shows the skill set that the students will have to continue to develop at university and also the student's passions, and it helps them stand out in what is a highly competitive environment of applying for university.

Case study 2 - STEAM projects

Esme Boyall - Lead Practitioner

STEM (Science, Technology, Engineering, and Maths) and latterly STEAM (Art has rightly been added) has been promoted for many years at Bosworth. It is one of the few organisations that fund cross-curricular work and helps students to see the connections across these (seemingly-disparate) subjects.

This funding has enabled us to host some spectacular events (robotics was a real highlight) as well as encourage girls to aspire to follow careers in this (previously male-dominated) world. It has also enabled us to connect Fourth Way projects like the Caterpillar Pre - Apprenticeship Programme with subjects outside of Engineering.

11th February 2019 – International day of women and girls in science

We need all hands on deck, and that means clearing hurdles for women and girls as they navigate careers in science, technology, engineering, and math.

— *Michelle Obama* —

AZ QUOTES

Bosworth Academy

TO ACHIEVE

STEM event a hit with students - Bosworth 'In the Loop' Newsletter

Year 7 and 8 students have been taking part in some exciting STEM (Science, Technology, Engineering, and Maths) workshops during March. This event was organised to make students aware of some of the amazing career options available to them in the future. We welcomed ambassadors from local company Caterpillar to talk to students about their engineering roles, careers routes, roles, and also about their own career paths.

The students were then given a real-life problem to solve. They were told about how farmers in Nepal needed to be able to transport tomatoes up and down the mountains, due to the isolated location of the farms and the poor road conditions.

The students were then split into teams and were asked to design a system to move trays of tomatoes from one end of the bench to the other using K'Nex pull systems. They had lots of fun using teamwork and communication skills to design effective methods of transport. At the end of the sessions, the students demonstrated how their strategies had worked and evaluated how effective they were.

STEM Cyber Day - 'In the Loop' Newsletter article

Computer Science students from Years 9 and 10 were put to the test this week as they tried to break the codes linked to cyber forensics in the latest STEM day. This was the third STEM day of the year where the students were tasked to do a digital treasure hunt, encryptions, and ethics which were all linked to the final activity of theoretically hacking a website to test its cyber security. Joining us for the day was Piers Prior from the Small Piece Trust which holds STEM days three times a week throughout the country.

Mr. Prior, who studied Automotive Material Engineering at Loughborough University, said it was "great that I now get to do this and help students consider the ethics of cyber security". The topics of cyber security and ethics make up a quarter of the GCSE Computer Science subject and it is hoped that the activities of the STEM day will be retained by the students when they reach their exams.

Case study 3 - Bosworth Productions

Becky Green, Brogan Penlington and Lisa Ravel - Performing Arts team

Bosworth Productions is a Year 8 enrichment programme that students choose to participate in for the full academic year. Originally the enrichment programme was Bosworth Theatre Company which looked specifically at developing Drama based skills as well as organising and putting on Drama performances. After the success of the Bosworth Theatre Company, Dance Leaders was also created to give students more exposure and a creative outlet within Dance too. Students took part in the school competition 'The Great Big Dance Off' for many years, competing against different schools within the region and sometimes making it through to the national finals also. Due to the success of both programmes, the uptake of Dance and Drama for GCSE improved. As a faculty, we identified that Music was not having the same exposure and therefore the enrichment evolved to become Bosworth Productions, encompassing all 3 disciplines of Dance, Drama and Music. The evolution of the enrichment programme means that students are now able to choose to study one discipline or collaborate between the different disciplines and can work towards creating full musicals. It gives students real-life experiences as each year we put on two different performances, a Christmas pantomime (that students re-write and contemporise), and then a Summer production that looks at performing a well-known musical, most recently Matilda.

We also make sure students have exposure to careers within Performance within Enrichment, for example, students have been to see the West End production of Matilda whilst working towards the performance to allow students to aspire to these roles. They have had workshops from leading providers in Leicestershire for

Performing Arts such as Studio 79 and also have the opportunity to showcase their work to parents and staff at matinee shows as well as at open evenings and in assemblies.

Every year we have over 60 students sign up to participate in the programme, showcasing how important the creative outlet is to our students. They develop their 6Cs immensely throughout the year and by the end all students have developed their agency by becoming more confident, creative, empowered, collaborative and clearer communicators. The programme creates a real buzz around performance within Key Stage Three, offering a place of belonging to our students. Quite often older students come to support and help lead the programme as they miss no longer being a part of it.

Chapter 7: Listen to, and act upon, the student voice

Jessica Maughan - student
Louise Holdback - Post 16 Team Leader

We have always valued and responded to what students have to say at Bosworth. This is important if you want to give students a sense of belonging and encourage them to participate in democratic society as adults. We have a number of student voice groups and use a variety of feedback mechanisms at class, faculty, key-stage, and whole-school level.

John Hattie talks about the importance of teachers being able to see the learning through the eyes of their students. Without this we can't begin to understand what misconceptions and barriers the students are experiencing. The best way to do this is through the student voice. A good teacher is always seeking feedback from their students about how they are feeling about their learning, the classroom environment, and their lives in general.

The initiatives we wanted to share here have been led by the students and by Louise Holdback in Post 16:

Case study 1: Student-led assemblies -
Jessica Maughan (student)

Here at Bosworth Academy, we are encouraged to find our own voice and to share our enthusiasm surrounding important topics and events. As students, we are guided to both reach our potential academically, and develop broader skills and attributes as well.

A major way in which life skills have been developed is through student-inspired and delivered assemblies. Across this academic year, students from all age groups have led nearly half of the assemblies, each based on a topic of passion and enthusiasm for students. This allows us to communicate pride in our cultures on important events in our calendars such as Diwali, Chinese New Year, or Advent, or promote inclusivity and diversity in our school when discussing Black History Month or LGBT+ History Month.

We have also had fantastic assemblies delivered on illnesses and the journeys associated with them to raise awareness of not what people are going through in our community. We have had students such as Kiya Kanani deliver inspiring assemblies on childhood cancer awareness after she herself was diagnosed with stage 4 Hodgkin's Lymphoma, making students aware of the signs as well as the fundraisers that she is hosting. Emily Wolfe delivered an assembly on her journey with Tourettes, and raised awareness of what living with Tourettes looked like and how it affected her daily life. Both of these assemblies made a great impact on many students and helped shine a light on some unspoken issues.

These assemblies are often presented in teams, with some even allowing multiple-year groups to come together and work on these projects, really building into a community spirit in our school.

By having students enthusiastically deliver these assemblies to our own peers, we not only teach and learn about crucial topics but also build upon our communication, character, citizenship, collaboration, creativity, and critical thinking in order to convey our message in the most effective manner. Building upon the 6 Cs here at Bosworth is a focus to help us leave school as well-rounded individuals.

This week, in accordance with International Women's Day, (which was on Tuesday 8 March) a Year 13 tutor group delivered three individual assemblies for each key stage. Creating separate assemblies enabled us to raise awareness appropriate for each year group and send the correct message for everyone. Our tutor group worked together to accumulate ideas and then branched out into teams to produce the individual assemblies.

By creating these videos, we ensured nobody would miss out on the important message of breaking the bias and barriers between genders. Key Stage Five assemblies went ahead as normal each day with a team of the Year 13 students independently delivering the assembly to our sixth-form cohort. The presentations included the key messages of International Women's Day as we raised awareness of prejudices in our society, but also provided resources so students could research the subject further themselves. We touched upon issues such as gender pay and status inequalities, and inspirational women who we should recognise as the role models they are.

All the messages we promoted played into this year's International Women's Day theme of 'break the bias' - working together to form an equal society, not only in our school but in the wider community too. In the end, even though International Women's Day is only celebrated one day a year, we should embody its message for all 365 days as we push toward a more inclusive society.

Case study 2: Student Voice at Post 16
Louise Holdback - Head of Post 16

We are always looking to engage student voice in the sixth form at Bosworth Academy. An 'open door' and 'solutions rather than problems' based policy is encouraged with students. A student voice group meets half termly to identify ways in which we could improve learning and teaching and the learning environment at Bosworth. Two representatives from each group attend meetings and agendas are created by students in response to issues raised by the student body as a whole. The representatives then discuss items with their tutor group and feedback to The Post 16 Team.

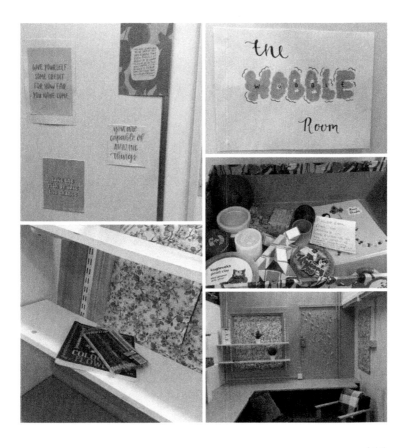

Alongside this initiative is the 'Open Door' policy where students are encouraged to share ideas that they think could improve their learning experience for students. An example of one of the successes of this initiative has been the creation of the wobble room. A learning space where students who are experiencing a 'wobble' and needing a little quiet time are encouraged to rebalance before returning to lessons. The room is resourced with self-help reference material and signposting to support providers.

Chapter 8: Assess Intelligently

Rick Moore - Key Stage Three Team Leader

We live in an age of endless data - much of this provided by high-stakes, standardised testing. Exam results have become the be-all and end-all of educational success. This makes no more sense than measuring a person's value simply on how much money they have or a country's success just by their GDP. Judging students solely by their grades is a crass and narrowing mechanism for determining their educational development and accomplishment. The holy grail of holistic education is finding a rigorous way of measuring all of the other competencies students need to thrive in the modern world that are currently missed by our exam system.

We are always looking for ways of measuring our students' progress accurately, but without increasing the amount of high-stakes testing they are subjected to. We use software such as PASS, Bedrock, and Maths Challenge to give us valuable insights into students' attitudes and learning behaviours - without putting students under undue pressure. Recently we have broadened our measures to include character and Michael Fullan's '6 Cs' and this is the case study we want to share with you here.

Case study - 6C student assessment, accreditation and rewards

Rick Moore - Head of Key Stage 3

The 6 Cs were developed by Micheal Fullan and represent the global competencies students need to thrive in the 21st century. We loved this work because it solved the problem of how we could measure what we truly valued, rather than just valuing what we could measure with conventional test data.

6C Global Competencies

Character
- Proactive stance toward life and learning to learn
- Grit, tenacity, perseverance and resilience
- Empathy, compassion and integrity in action

Citizenship
- A global perspective
- Commitment to human equity and well-being through empathy and compassion for diverse values and world views
- Genuine interest in human and environmental sustainability
- Solving ambiguous and complex problems in the real world to benefit citizens

Collaboration
- Working interdependently as a team
- Interpersonal and team-related skills
- Social, emotional, and intercultural skills
- Managing team dynamics and challenges

Communication
- Communication designed for audience and impact
- Message advocates a purpose and makes an impact
- Reflection to further develop and improve communication
- Voice and identity expressed to advance humanity

Creativity
- Economic and social entrepreneurialism
- Asking the right inquiry questions
- Pursuing and expressing novel ideas and solutions
- Leadership to turn ideas into action

Critical Thinking
- Evaluating information and arguments
- Making connections and identifying patterns
- Meaningful knowledge construction
- Experimenting, reflecting and taking action on ideas in the real world

OECD

The 6 Cs have become our way of tracking and measuring all the aspects of agency that exam data misses. We are now able to assess the true impact of our curriculum intent and discover whether our students are really developing their agency during their years at Bosworth.

Character for Learning - for use from August 2018

Character for Learning (CfL)	Descriptor
2 (GOLD)	Always highly self-motivated and proactive in lessons. Has high expectations for the quality of work that they want to produce and regularly demonstrates a growth mindset by completing all forms of work to the best of their ability thanks to their persistence, dedication and effort.
1 (SILVER)	Often highly self-motivated and proactive in lessons. Regularly completes work to a good standard that is beyond minimum expectation for their ability. Usually demonstrates persistence, dedication and effort when taking on challenging work.
0 (BRONZE)	Regularly completes work to an acceptable standard without additional encouragement from staff to engage in the lesson and remain on task.
-1	Often requires encouragement from staff to engage in lesson activities and remain on task. Often fails to complete work to an acceptable standard and may have a tendency to be distracted by or to distract others.
-2	Regularly demonstrates a very low level of motivation and does not proactively engage in lessons. Shows little or no resilience when taking on challenging work and regularly fails to complete work to an acceptable standard. Has a detrimental impact upon the learning of others.

In order to assess our students' progress in developing their 6C skills, we have created our Bosworth Colours. The Bosworth Colours is a series of challenges that students have to overcome. As students complete the challenges they win their colours' badge for each of the 6C areas. The challenges in each area have been constructed to ensure students fully develop the competencies that prepare them for the test of life (and life is a test isn't it?) rather than just a life of tests - who takes exams after they leave education?

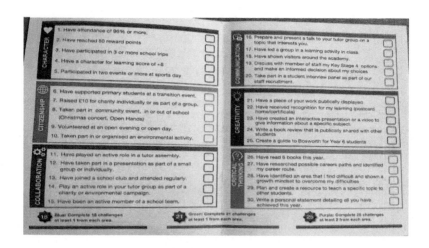

CHARACTER	1. Have attendance of 96% or more. 2. Have reached 50 reward points 3. Have participated in 3 or more school trips 4. Have a character for learning score of +8 5. Participated in two events or more at sports day
CITIZENSHIP	6. Have supported primary students at a transition event. 7. Raised £10 for charity individually or as part of a group. 8. Taken part in community event, in or out of school (Christmas concert, Open Hands) 9. Volunteered at an open evening or open day. 10. Taken part in or organised an environmental activity.
COLLABORATION	11. Have played an active role in a tutor assembly. 12. Have taken part in a presentation as part of a small group or individually. 13. Have joined a school club and attended regularly. 14. Play an active role in your tutor group as part of a charity or environmental campaign. 15. Have been an active member of a school team.
COMMUNICATION	16. Prepare and present a talk to your tutor group on a topic that interests you. 17. Have led a group in a learning activity in class. 18. Have shown visitors around the academy. 19. Discuss with member of staff my Key Stage 4 options and make an informed decision about my choices 20. Take part in a student interview panel as part of our staff recruitment.
CREATIVITY	21. Have a piece of your work publically displayed. 22. Have received recognition for my learning (postcard, home/certificate) 23. Have created an interactive presentation or a video to give information about a specific subject. 24. Write a book review that is publically shared with other students 25. Create a guide to Bosworth for Year 6 students
CRITICAL THINKING	26. Have read 5 books this year. 27. Have researched possible careers paths and identified my career route. 28. Have identified an area that I find difficult and shown a growth mindset to overcome my difficulties 29. Plan and create a resource to teach a specific topic to other students. 30. Write a personal statement detailing all you have achieved this year.

18 Blue: Complete 18 challenges at least 1 from each area.

21 Green: Complete 21 challenges at least 1 from each area.

25 Purple: Complete 25 challenges at least 2 from each area.

Colours Evening - In the Loop Newsletter article

On Tuesday 5 July we invited students across Years 7-10, and their friends and families, to celebrate their success in achieving in the 6Cs Colours. The awards evening opened with a montage of photos of students set to the music of Estonia's Eurovision Song Contest entry, 'Hope' by Stefan. As Mr. Brown highlighted in his talk afterward, the lyrics "the future still remains our own" rings true in the

current climate, as it is up to us to make our own future in this unpredictable world.

Following talks from Mrs. Duncan and Mr. Moore, certificates and badges were handed out to students who received three or more stamps in a 6C category. Further rewards were handed out to students who got over 150 reward points and received a Headteacher medal. Students were then invited to pose with their prizes on the red carpet outside the Main Hall. Well done to all students - you definitely deserve the break over the summer holiday.

Chapter 9: Develop your Professional Capital

Liam Grest - PE Team Leader

All the research agrees that developing high-quality teachers is the key to student success. In their book 'Professional Capital' (6) Professors Hargreaves and Fullan argue that the way to do this is by 'getting the best people, getting them to work together, and getting them to stay'. They sum this up in the formula HC + SC + DC = PC, which stands for: Human Capital plus Social Capital plus Decisional Capital equals Professional Capital.

They argue that you attract the best people (human capital) by providing decent pay, job status and security, good working conditions and union protection. You should look for candidates who are well-qualified - but also exhibit good social skills and the ability to work in a team. Most importantly they need to exhibit a sense of purpose and moral drive.

They assert that you encourage teachers to work together (social capital) by developing learning communities which are bottom-up, autonomous, and give people a big voice in whole-school decision-making. We want teachers who feel responsible rather than accountable, and who see teaching as a vocation and not a job. This can be nurtured through allowing genuine debate and discussion and empowering staff to align their practice with their values. You cannot force teachers to adopt a new approach - they have to be persuaded by reason. Forced initiatives tend to flounder under indifference, or even deliberate sabotage - coercion leads to subversion.

Social capital can make an enormous difference to the efficacy of your teachers - akin to getting your staff to work as a team rather than as individual stars. John Hattie also places 'collective teacher efficacy' at the top of his 256 factors related to student achievement in his work on 'Visible Learning' (7).

Hargreaves and Fullan also argue that getting people to stay (decisional capital) is crucial. Teachers only really hit their stride after 6-8 years and so, if you want to reap the benefit of their experience, you need to hold onto them by treating them with dignity and respect. This experience enables teachers to make the right calls more often when the situation is not clear - hence 'decisional capital'.
Given the hundreds of interactions teachers can have with students and staff every day, this decision-making ability is invaluable.

One of our main retention strategies is through staff well-being initiatives and that is what we want to showcase in this chapter.

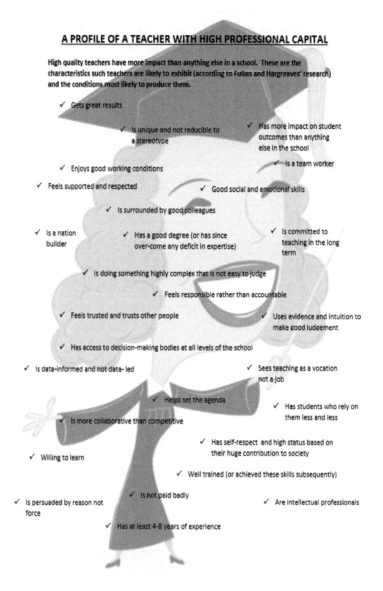

A PROFILE OF A TEACHER WITH HIGH PROFESSIONAL CAPITAL

High quality teachers have more impact than anything else in a school. These are the characteristics such teachers are likely to exhibit (according to Fullan and Hargreaves' research) and the conditions most likely to produce them.

- ✓ Gets great results
- ✓ Is unique and not reducible to a stereotype
- ✓ Has more impact on student outcomes than anything else in the school
- ✓ Enjoys good working conditions
- ✓ Is a team worker
- ✓ Feels supported and respected
- ✓ Good social and emotional skills
- ✓ Is surrounded by good colleagues
- ✓ Is a nation builder
- ✓ Has a good degree (or has since over-come any deficit in expertise)
- ✓ Is committed to teaching in the long term
- ✓ Is doing something highly complex that is not easy to judge
- ✓ Feels responsible rather than accountable
- ✓ Feels trusted and trusts other people
- ✓ Uses evidence and intuition to make good judgement
- ✓ Has access to decision-making bodies at all levels of the school
- ✓ Is data-informed and not data-led
- ✓ Sees teaching as a vocation not a job
- ✓ Helps set the agenda
- ✓ Has students who rely on them less and less
- ✓ Is more collaborative than competitive
- ✓ Has self-respect and high status based on their huge contribution to society
- ✓ Willing to learn
- ✓ Well trained (or achieved these skills subsequently)
- ✓ Is not paid badly
- ✓ Is persuaded by reason not force
- ✓ Are intellectual professionals
- ✓ Has at least 4-8 years of experience

Case study - Staff well-being strategies

Liam Grest - Head of PE

Looking after our staff is a top priority at Bosworth. According to the research in 'Professional Capital' teachers only really hit their stride as professionals after eight years and so it is imperative we support them (and all our staff) if we are to reap the benefits of their experience and judgement in the long term.

One of the ways we have done this is through the introduction of 'Well-being Wednesday'. After-school meetings on this day are discouraged and a variety of staff come together to partake in physical activity. For example, there are staff clubs in:

- Running
- Yoga
- Circuit training and other uses of school facilities
- Badminton
- Table tennis

We also introduced three morning swims at our on-site pool. Staff can access the sessions free of charge and start their day with a swim. Active travel is also encouraged and an area in the school greenhouse was designed to allow the safe storage of bicycles and a staff changing room, with lockers to allow staff to keep their kit safe.

The benefit of a thriving well-being programme for staff is that it brings staff together outside of the classrooms and across faculties.

Links are made between staff who could otherwise be simply ships in the night as they pass on the corridors. 'Well-being Wednesday' also gives a day that is largely protected from an after-school meeting so staff can join in one of the range of activities or simply end the day knowing that it is their time. The teamship and togetherness can only go to enhance the morale of the whole staff and create a cohesive team who are more

likely to look out for and after each-other. A further well-being

strategy that has been successfully implemented over recent years is the school's involvement in the *Movember Schools* challenge. Staff and students are invited to grow a moustache or 'move for Movember' - pledging to move 60km throughout the month in honour of the 60 males who die by suicide each hour globally. Throughout the campaigns of 2020 and 2021, as a school, we have raised over £17,000 and seen a large number of staff members get involved and pledge to run.

Chapter 10: Bringing it all together

Steve Hall - REALiFE Coordinator

All of this work culminated in the creation of the REAL LiFE curriculum in 2020. This was particularly inspired by our visits to the XP School in Doncaster and combines all of the Fourth Way principles described above in a fully integrated, multi-disciplinary curriculum. It has been by far our most ambitious venture to date and has required massive amounts of planning and training to implement.

Integrating a cross-curricular course into a mainstream school is akin to rebuilding a plane whilst you are still in the air. Training staff up to this entirely new way of teaching, whilst they are still delivering conventional courses as well, is not an easy proposition. However, the engagement and agency exhibited by the students in these lessons make all of the headaches worthwhile and we have been careful to plan that the model is sustainable in the long term.

Steve Hall has led this extremely exciting work and has been indefatigable. As a result of all of his team's endeavours the REALiFE curriculum is now being rolled out successfully right across the MAT, in Years 7 and 8 as well as in our primary schools. Steve outlines this work below.

Case Study: The 'REALiFE' Curriculum

Life doesn't always fit neatly into isolated subject areas, yet this mainly logistical solution still dominates our education systems, often at the expense of genuinely deep and personalised learning.

The Real LiFE Curriculum has been designed by experts from across the LiFE MAT who have looked at research conducted by world-leading organisations about how education can best prepare students to meet the needs of the 21st century. But we want our students to do more than simply be ready to cope with the future…we want them to be able to shape it!

To do this our students need to have **agency**, and the OECD helped to determine our collective understanding of what this means.

"Student agency…is rooted in the belief that students have the ability and the will to positively influence their own lives and the world around them. Student agency is defined as the capacity to set a goal, reflect and act responsibly to effect change."
Source: https://www.oecd.org/education/2030-project/teaching-and-learning/learning/student-agency/

Our schools have always had students that fit this description, but the key question we considered was, "Can we empower more of our students to demonstrate higher levels of Student Agency more often?"

For our students to have the genuine will to make a positive difference we knew that our Real LiFE Curriculum would need to be relevant, interesting, and engaging. To do this we firstly make sure that everything in our curriculum is applied to and immerses the students in its real-life context. This stops the students from wondering what the point of learning about a particular topic is.

We thought long and hard about what would be interesting and engaging for the students to learn about, and how we would incorporate it into the curriculum. The problem facing all curriculum designers is that a balance needs to be struck between the knowledge and skills that are expected to be taught in order for students and schools to meet accountability measures, and the diverse range of interests that capture the imagination of our students. In the Real Life Curriculum, we solve this through **CREW** and multi-disciplinary **Missions**, and the main strategy that allows both of these features to develop student agency and empower students to take greater ownership of their learning is the use of our **Critique** protocol to help students self and peer assess their progress towards **Visible Success Criteria**.

CREW stands for Coaching, Reflection, Enrichment, and Wellbeing. It is a daily timetabled session that is fundamental to building the levels of student agency that we desire. Students are encouraged to take more ownership of their own progress and learning in the Real LiFE Curriculum and we are able to prepare and support our students to do this in CREW sessions. On a Monday morning, our students are coached by the CREW leader to set their goals for the week ahead. In total, our students set four goals, one each for reading, maths, their current mission, and a personal goal. They need to follow the SMART principle (Specific, Measurable, Agreed, Realistic, Time), and once set, the students plan their use of the personalised learning time that is available during subsequent CREW sessions by outlining how they intend to meet these goals by the end of the week. This is recorded on a template that is uploaded to Google Classroom as an assignment which enables the CREW Leader to easily review and monitor student progress.

Weekly Goals

Remember to make your goals SMART:

S = Specific. Don't be vague…try to say exactly what you plan to accomplish.

M = Measurable. You can choose to measure how much you want to achieve by time or the number of tasks/exercises/pages you are aiming to complete.

A = Agreed - make sure that this is something your CREW leader will approve of!

R = Realistic - don't be over or under-ambitious. The goals should be a challenge but not something that is impossible!

T = Time - give yourself a time limit and a deadline otherwise you will find that they will drift!

My goals for the week (Reading, Maths, Mission, and Personal)

- The book I will be reading this week is…
- The Maths topic that I plan to improve my understanding of is…
- In my mission I need to…
- My personal goal is to…

Personalised Learning Opportunities	What I plan to do in the Personalised Learning Time that is available that day (be very specific and detailed about your mission and personalised work)
Monday	1. I will set my goals for the week 2. I will use any remaining time to…
Tuesday	
Wednesday	
Thursday	
Friday	1. I will review how effective my goals were in the table below 2. I will use any remaining time to…

Friday Goal Review (complete the table below at the end of the week)

	What did I achieve in relation to this goal?	What should my goal for this be next week?
Reading		
Hegarty Maths		
My Mission		
My Personal Goal		

To support this process, we put together a Personalised Learning Menu that points the students towards the many online learning platforms and resources that most schools already have available but are often under-utilised. In our LiFE MAT schools, we use Accelerated Reader to support the Reading goal and Hegarty Maths to support the Maths Goal.

For each mission, we publish a student guide with visible success criteria to help inform the mission goal (more on that later). While our menu highlights learning platforms from a range of subjects, as well as opportunities to enter national competitions to help inform the personal goal. We have two simple rules for the personal goal in addition to it meeting the SMART principle. Firstly, it needs to be something that you can work on safely in a normal classroom, and secondly, it must be something that can be worked towards without disturbing others. Of course, students are able to set themselves additional personal goals that they can work towards in their own time at home, and many of our students do…yes, some of our students have been setting themselves extra homework!

At the end of the week, the students reflect on their progress and upload basic evidence in the form of photos and screenshots which helps the CREW leader to monitor how successfully they have used their personalised learning time as well as to prepare the students for the following week's cycle of goal setting.

In our multidisciplinary **Missions,** students are immersed in a real-world issue and are challenged to come up with a response to that issue by developing a final product that is showcased via an event or exhibition where selected members of the public (such as their peers, family, and industry experts) are invited. Our students do still take tests and other assessments to demonstrate their understanding, but the public showcasing of work gives this a far more powerful experience that is much more relevant to real life.

We wanted to ensure that our students would continue to benefit from teaching by subject specialists, and also be prepared to select from an equally broad range of examination subjects as the students who follow a 'traditional' curriculum. The themes for our

multidisciplinary missions were decided by consulting curriculum leaders from all of our subject areas, as well as through listening to students and staff. We were inspired by the approach of the World's Largest Lesson (https://worldslargestlesson.globalgoals.org/) to use the UN Global Goals as the umbrella theme for our missions. The Global Goals are often described as a 'to do' list for our planet. We want our students to make a positive difference in the world around them so it became the perfect guide to inform our planning.

To decide which of the Global Goals we would use in our missions, representatives of each subject area looked at our existing curriculum maps to establish where there might be possible opportunities to build on each other's teaching. Relatively quickly this allowed us to settle on the following missions for our Year 7 students:

- Who am I? - Global Goals 4 (Quality Education) and 10 (Reduced inequalities)
- Climate Action - Global Goal 13
- Good Health and Wellbeing - Global Goal 4

We deliver one mission per term over an 8-12 week period to ensure that students are able to go deep in their learning without drowning! Missions start with each subject providing an immersive experience that helps bring the issue to life from the perspective of their subject area. We have added Virtual Reality to our range of immersive experiences, but are mindful not to use technology at the expense of the many perfectly good immersive experiences that schools have always delivered both in and out of the classroom such as role play tasks, trips, and visits.

The final product for the mission is broken down into milestone tasks with the subject teacher deemed best suited to overseeing each milestone and taking responsibility for its delivery through their timetabled lessons. The subject specialists agree on when they should do this and are also responsible for providing feedback to the students about the evidence they submit towards this milestone task. All of the milestone tasks are set as assignments on a Google Classroom which means that all of the subject teachers, as well as the CREW leader, are able to see the progress of each student in real time.

Throughout the year our subject specialists do still teach other topics that don't fit authentically into any of the Missions. It is the responsibility of each teacher to manage their teaching time through medium and long-term planning so that they teach the Mission milestone tasks at the appropriate time as well as follow the discrete Schemes of Learning from their Curriculum maps in their remaining contact time.

While CREW and Missions provide the structure for student agency to be developed, it is the use of our protocol for **Critique** using the **Visible Success Criteria** for reference that really equips students with the skills needed to make a positive difference to themselves and the world around them. Humans are brilliantly adept at completing tasks that they deem necessary but do they always complete them to the best possible standard and do they inherently know what that best possible standard might look like? The need to provide leadership and support to others is also really highly valued in society, but how do we ensure that the feedback we give to others is delivered in a way that is useful without leading to offence and embarrassment?

We were inspired by Ron Berger's rules of Critique, in that it should be kind, specific, and helpful. Experienced classroom practitioners can recount endless examples of students either being too nice or too generic when asked to self and peer assess (not particularly useful or specific) or being too subjectively harsh (unkind) which can be catastrophic to a productive learning environment! A third outcome is often one that is the most common - students being too scared to give feedback for fear of failure because they don't understand what the next steps for improvement could be. Our solution to this has been to carefully consider what success in a task looks like by providing clear

Visible Success Criteria to accompany tasks, and to coach the students to communicate their **Critique** by using the following sentence stems; "I like…I notice…I wonder…".

The Visible Success Criteria are presented as Bronze, Silver, Gold, and Platinum steps and are written in the form of "I can" statements to provide the students with positive actions that they can do. We use the Hess Cognitive Rigor Matrix (https://www.karin-hess.com/cognitive-rigor-and-dok) as a reference tool when planning to ensure depth, rigour, and challenge, but in simple terms, the bronze objective is the minimum acceptable response that often involves presentation of key facts, with silver, gold, and platinum scaffolding the next step actions needed for the students to demonstrate an increasing depth of the application/evaluation of knowledge.

The table below shows the Visible Success Criteria that were used as part of the Climate Action mission in a joint milestone shared between Maths and Science.

Milestone 3: I can explain why plants are so important <u>and</u> use mathematical calculations to produce a carbon-reducing plan for the school

	Bronze	Silver	Gold	Platinum
Area (Maths)	I can measure lengths using a variety of different measurements and tools	I can calculate the area of rectangles and triangles within the environment of my school	I can calculate the area of composite shapes to work out the areas of unused space around the school	I can solve problems using area involving percentages, costs to produce a plan on carbon sinks around our school

Plants & Soil (Science)	I can identify at least one type of plant that would improve the ability of our school site to reduce Carbon and be able to suggest an appropriate location (based on the type of soil) where we should attempt to grow it.	In addition to Bronze I can attempt to grow my own plants from seed and be able to describe the process of how they are able to grow (germination).	In addition to Silver I can explain how to conduct an experiment to compare the different types of soil for growing plants.	In addition to Gold I can use the data from this experiment to justify the type of soil we should use to grow plants as part of our carbon reduction plan.

The example above highlights one of the many benefits we have experienced since introducing the Real LiFE Curriculum. Staff from the full range of subject specialisms are collaborating to an extent that has simply not been possible before. This has highlighted areas of overlap and inconsistency that previously existed, one of many examples being the way that historically Maths, Science, and Geography have used data and graphs. Our staff has been able to learn from each other and are now able to identify and exploit opportunities to build on each other's work.

It is however the positive impact that the Real LiFE Curriculum has had on the students that have given us the impetus to move forward in this way. Our groups have consistently shown higher levels of attendance and had fewer negative behaviour incidents which supports the perception of teachers that these students are more engaged in their learning than students who had followed a 'traditional' curriculum. They have used the personalised learning time in CREW to great effect, with numerous students choosing to learn additional languages while others have embraced learning technologies by using online tutorials to learn how to code mobile apps and create virtual reality experiences. We have also had a significant number of students using this time to enter national competitions such as the BP Ultimate STEM challenge and the HG Wells short story competition. The comparative attainment data between the Real LiFE Curriculum students and those following the 'traditional' curriculum in areas such as reading, maths, and science has also been very favourable. By the end of the first year of the Real LiFE Curriculum, a significant number of students increased their reading age by more than two years with some increasing as much as four years!

In the classroom, it is clear that the Real LiFE Curriculum's focus on the critique by using the visible success criteria for reference means that the students submit higher quality work and are able to generate their own next-step feedback. Finally, the experience these students are gaining through the public nature of the final products is giving them the confidence and articulacy they need to take positive action to improve the world around them. If we can empower more students to be like this our future will be in safe hands!

Chapter 11: The quality of education

How we learned to stop worrying and love OFSTED
When we started the Fourth Way work it felt very counter-cultural. However, when Ofsted, quite rightly, started to focus on the 'quality of education' in schools and to question the exam factory system that had emerged during the second and third way in England we felt ourselves to be in a position of real strength. Given it was something we had been working on for years,

A BROAD AND BALANCED KS3 CURRICULUM – BOSWORTH ACADEMY 2017-18

SUBJECT CURRICULUM	EXPEDITIONARY CURRICULUM PROJECTS	PROJECT-BASED LEARNING CURRICULUM
ENGLISH MATHS SCIENCE PE HUMANITIES PERFORMANCE - ROTATION ADT - ROTATION COMPUTING/IT - ROTATION ENRICHMENT (SEE BELOW)	VINEGAR MAKING ART INSTALLATION LANDROVER/TRIUMPH SPORT EDUCATION UNIT PLANTING THE FUTURE FOREST FRENCH CHRISTMAS CARDS 6TH FORM CAFÉ BOSWORTH THEATRE COMPANY PIZZA MATHS COKE CAN MATHS STEM-BUILDING ROCKET CARS STOCKING MAKING LUCHA LIBRA MASKS CREATING AN ART EXHIBITION SPACE	MATHS: SELLOTAPE PACKAGING, POP ART ENGLISH: MYTHICAL CREATURES, THE GOTHIC TRADITION, CHARITY CAMPAIGNS ICT: STEM AND FEMALE PARTICIPATION SCIENCE: BIODIESEL, PERFUMERY PE: COUCH TO 5K, SPORTS LEADERSHIP, ACTIVE LIFE-STYLES AND FIRST AID CULTURAL: CHRISTMAS CONCERT, MUSIC VIDEOS, PERFORMANCE ETC ADT: ALL SUBJECTS ARE PROJECT-BASED LEARNING HUMANITIES: ENGLISH CIVIL WAR TUTOR: NEWS REPORT
ENRICHMENT CURRICULUM	4TH WAY NATIONAL CURRICULUM	COMMUNITY CURRICULUM
YEAR 7: - MUSICAL THEATRE, PINHOLE PHOTOGRAPHY, ENAMELLING, LET'S COOK! STREET DANCE, FILM MAKING, UP-CYCLING, GARDEN DESIGNS, FORENSIC SCIENCE, THE ART OF ARGUING. ADD FRENCH/SPANISH. YEAR 8: - THE BOSWORTH THEATRE COMPANY, STARTING A BUSINESS, CONSTRUCTION, MEDIA STUDIES, DEBATING, SPORTS LEADERSHIP, EXT.LANGUAGES.	MATHS: APPLY MATHEMATICAL KNOWLEDGE TO OTHER SUBJECTS. SCIENCE: STUDY ENVIRONMENT INCLUDING ECO-SYSTEMS, POLLUTION, RECYCLING, CLIMATE CHANGE, ENERGY. GEOGRAPHY: MAPS, ATLASES, FIELDWORK AND THE ENVIRONMENT. HISTORY: LOCAL HISTORY AND SITES AND CONNECTIONS WITH NATIONAL AND INTERNATIONAL HISTORY. PE: OUTDOOR AND ADVENTUROUS ACTIVITIES. COMPUTING: APPLY COMPUTATIONAL THINKING TO A RANGE OF OTHER SUBJECTS	COMMUNITY GARDEN HENRICHMENT FRENCH PARTNERSHIP DESFORD LIBRARY BARNS CHARITY FIELD DESFORD FC FILM STUDIO MUSIC STUDIO CHRISTMAS EXTRAVAGANZA ADT PRIMARY CREATIVITY
CROSS-CURRICULAR PROJECTS	SKILLS & CHARACTER CURRICULUM	EXTRA-CURRICULUM
YEAR 7 – LEICESTER FOREST –MATHS, HUMANITIES, PE, ADT YEAR 8 – ENVIRONMENT – MATHS, ADT, ENGLISH, HUMANITIES, SCIENCE, DANCE & BUSINESS YEAR 9 – THE COLD WAR – MATHS, ADT & HUMANITIES MAP ROOM – ALL YEARS – BUSINESS, ENGLISH, SEN, EPQ, GEOG & HISTORY	ACHIEVERS ADOPT A CHARITY WORLD CHALLENGE	SEE TIME-TABLE
		EDUCATIONAL VISITS CURRICULUM
		SEE PRINT-OUT

135

Amanda Spielman's insistence on a 'broad and balanced' curriculum was music to our ears.

When Ofsted's 3'I' model was introduced we quickly set to work adapting this framework to our own practices and values. This led to the creation of our whole-school curriculum model which distilled all of our best practice and formalised our Fourth Way approach to education. It also drew heavily on the OECD 2030 Learning Framework which fitted perfectly with our Fourth Way philosophy.

Bosworth Academy
Whole-School Curriculum Planning 2022

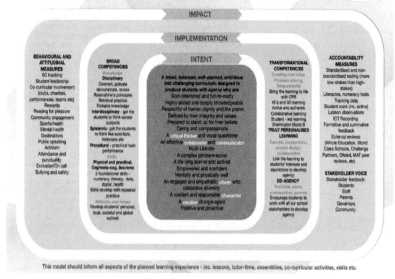

This model should inform all aspects of the planned learning experience - inc. lessons, tutor-time, assemblies, co-curricular activities, visits etc.

In this model, student agency is placed at the heart of our curriculum intent (the 6Cs are in white), and local and community education is also embedded throughout. The model also bakes in a truly personalised approach to curriculum implementation and emphasises the importance of embracing all of our stakeholders to enrich our provision. Intelligent assessment is woven into the curriculum impact section to ensure we are really developing student agency across the school. CPR stands for Creativity, Problem-solving, and Responsibility - which fits our motto of bringing learning to life.

We then asked subject leaders to articulate their curriculum stories in alignment with this model. We defined the story as **what** they teach, the plot as **when** they teach it, and the narrative as **why** they teach it. Here is the PE story for example:

Physical Education Curriculum Narrative 2022

Key: **Intent - what is the vision?** *Implementation - how is it taught?* <u>Impact - is it working?</u>

Physical Education is taught as a core curriculum with students completing two one-hour lessons per week from Year 7 through to Year 11. Students also have the option to select GCSE Physical Education from Year 9 through to Year 11 and then A Level Physical Education in Years 12 and 13.

The core Physical Education journey aims to develop students who are **multi-literate (health and physicality), demonstrate excellent character, and are inspired to discover, and reach their personal best.** The key goal is to prepare **lifelong learners and participants in physical activity.** From Year 7 to Year 9, students are taught in a series of 4-week (8 lesson), units of work that are built upon year on year.

In the foundation part of the curriculum in Year 7, students complete *a series of introductory units into activity areas (handling invasion games, net-wall games, swimming, for example).* This is to give students an appreciation of how to play general games that they develop in later years; *net-wall games later become a badminton unit from Year 8.*

Our 2022 curriculum review in Physical Education intends to move <u>assessment more towards our 6Cs and skills that are transferable between units and across the school,</u> thus moving away from a more *traditional sport-specific skill and fitness approach.* Moving into Years 10 and 11 the unit content becomes more personalised with students being offered choices. In Year 10, *the groups will work in a set space and tailor the activity to the needs of the group, for instance - Dome: Handball.* Moving into Year 11 the plan, disrupted by Covid, was to offer a pathway choice whereby students self-select a *performance, recreational, health, or fitness pathway. Lessons are then delivered in a way to suit the group and the facility.* **The rationale for this is to give autonomy of choice in their final year of core Physical Education whilst also giving a physical, mental and social release from exam stresses.**

The three-year GCSE curriculum begins with a long-term project with students completing a *personal exercise programme (PEP) whereby theory, which will later be built upon in Years 10 and 11, will be learned.* The aim of this is to *personalise the learning* of the students by asking them to develop their fitness in a way to improve their own sporting performance. Complex theory is covered in this process: *aspects of a warm-up and cool down; monitoring heart rate and understanding data; assessing fitness; planning a specific training program and carrying out this plan.* By the end of the project, <u>students have an appreciation and understanding of the rationale of testing fitness and how to plan and implement a training programme.</u>

In Years 10 and 11 students complete the PEP coursework, going into greater analysis and evaluation of performance and factors surrounding training planning. Students also study three main concept areas: physiological factors, psychological factors, and socio-cultural factors relating to physical education and sport. This is delivered by a variety of teaching methods - teacher delivery, research task, independent study, and group presentation.

The two-year A Level builds on knowledge, skills, and understanding of the GCSE Physical Education course. The same three concepts remain, namely physiological factors, psychological factors, and socio-cultural factors with students deepening their grasp of the concepts. Lessons are delivered through teacher delivery, research task, independent study, and group presentation.

Excellent outcomes show a significant impact on the quality of teaching and learning but also student-teacher relationships are outstanding with students feeling valued and appreciated and many going on student Sports Science at University.

We contribute to the whole-school cross-curriculum through our powerful Leicester Forest work in Year 7 where students complete a historical cross-country run and take part in a traditional Hereswode Games of poachers/gamekeepers. In Year 8, as part of the environment, all students complete an 8-mile walk across open countryside to Thornton Reservoir - giving our urban students appreciation and awareness of their local and very rural environment. We also have a thriving extra-curricular sporting offer where students can take part recreationally or as part of school teams in inter-school fixtures.

PE also designed an innovative assessment matrix that balanced knowledge, skills, and the 6Cs to determine the students' working at grades. This felt much more accurate and useful than judging such novice learners on academic levels alone. Here the 6Cs have equal weighting with knowledge and skills when determining student progress. We now use this approach in all of our Key Stage Three subjects:

Core Physical Education Assessment Criteria

Curriculum Intent

To develop students who are multi-literate (health and physically), demonstrate excellent character and are inspired to discover, and reach their personal best. To prepare lifelong learners and participants in physical activity.

Physical Literacy

Individuals who are physically literate move with competence and confidence in a wide variety of physical activities in multiple environments that benefit the healthy development of the whole person.

Our only concern was that when Ofsted came in they would not share our commitment to holistic education. We had heard so much about their adherence to a 'knowledge-rich' curriculum (often another way of saying: 'we teach to the test') and were naturally anxious that they would take a dim view of our broader definition of what a 'quality' education looks like.

As it turned out, however, we needn't have worried. When we were inspected in 2022 Ofsted was extremely impressed by our genuine commitment to a broad and balanced curriculum and judged the 'quality of education' at our school to be outstanding.

**Excerpt from Inspection report: Bosworth Academy
14 and 15 June 2022**

Pupils contribute to their community through a range of projects and charity work. They learn to be good citizens and

play an active role in their school, in society, and in the world. Students in the sixth form help younger pupils to improve their reading. Pupil groups lead assemblies on matters that are important to them. The curriculum helps pupils to develop the skills and attributes to flourish as citizens through the '6 Cs' (collaboration, citizenship, communication, critical thinking, creativity, and character). Parents and pupils value these opportunities.

The inspectors were impressed with all of our curriculum leaders after their 'deep dives', and were particularly complimentary about PE in the final report:

Leaders want pupils to achieve academic excellence and develop their character. They know that they must make the most of every lesson to achieve this ambition. For example, in physical education (PE), pupils learn to work well in a team, as well as learn PE-specific skills and knowledge of the subject. Leaders have thought carefully about what pupils already know and what they should learn in each subject. Leaders have made sure that learning builds steadily. They have made sure that pupils have plenty of chances to practise what they have learned.

Dispelling the 'knowledge-rich' myth about Ofsted felt very significant because it demonstrated that we needn't see Ofsted as an impediment to providing an authentic and holistic education for all of our students. In fact, astonishingly, (given that they were once the main drivers of the exam factory system), you could argue that Ofsted has now become an agent for holistic and mindful education. Would schools now be discussing the curriculum (rather than just PIXL and exam results) without Ofsted's new 'Quality of Education' focus?

Conclusion

Without wishing to sound too melodramatic, our Fourth Way journey has often felt like an odyssey in the epic sense of the word. Just as Odysseus overcame many obstacles on his 10-year journey back to Ithaca, we too faced a decade of challenges and setbacks before we reached our desired destination.

OK, we didn't encounter Cyclops, but we did have to convince a lot of people that our approach wouldn't be a distraction from ensuring student outcomes. This was despite our repeated assurance that The Fourth Way was based upon research into the highest-achieving educational systems around the world. Our mantra during this time was, 'start with the Whole Education Network, finish with PIXL'.

We also bit off more than we could chew with some projects (especially the ones that could have been expensive). We never did get adult community classes running again or build the community skateboard plaza - although we liked the student design:

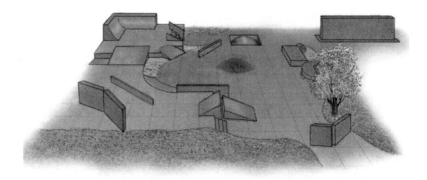

We also saw successful projects wind down or close down (the new build on top of the arboretum was particularly dispiriting!) and had ideas that are yet to take off - (see 'Bosworth Big Ideas' - in the Appendix for example). Indeed, without the epic resilience and perseverance of key members of staff going repeatedly above and beyond, we would never have embedded the Fourth Way into our culture so successfully.

They say it takes 10 years to change a culture and the nine principles described in this book have clearly become part of our 'DNA'. Our work has moved from the margins of the school to being integral to everything we do. The 6 Cs and student agency are now embedded in our everyday practice rather than being just an occasional add-on. We are also seeing innovative and inspiring leadership in all of these areas and this is having a tremendously positive effect on our overall educational provision. The fact that Fourth Way leadership is now widely distributed across the school also bodes well for future sustainability.

It was a gamble for a mainstream school like ours to attempt such a counter-cultural experiment on top of all the demands placed on staff in the modern era, but we are very glad that we took it. We were not an amazing 'School 21' or' XP School' that was set up to teach holistically from the start; back in 2013, we were a fairly typical secondary comprehensive - albeit with an innovative past. Nevertheless, our staff rose to the challenge magnificently. Our Fourth-Way work has enriched the experiences of our students, aligned staff with their values, and strengthened our entire learning community enormously.

The Fourth Way attempts to combine the best of old and new practices in global education. As such, some of the projects which came out of this philosophy were old-school classics that had gone out of fashion (the French Exchange, cross-country runs, the school garden, etc.) as well as new ideas around student agency, digital technology and communication, and the 6 Cs. This blend of old and new both respects the past and embraces the future.

For a vision to work, you need to synchronise all of your other practices around it. All of the principles above were designed to reinforce our ultimate aim of developing student agency. We want students to take control of their lives and shape the future, rather than just react to it. After a review by Challenge Partners in May 2022, they commented that our students were "The most active and engaged learners we've seen in a school this academic year" and that "there is a strong focus on developing student character and agency, to make a difference to their lives, not for Ofsted".

Almost all of the case studies in this book are, of course, examples of active learning. Modern education has become terribly passive. There is the apocryphal story of the photography course in America where none of the students took a photo - they just studied photographic theory instead. It may not be true but it sounds about right these days.

The picture on the front of this book was inspired by a Mick Waters' talk. In it, he said that, whilst he goes into schools hoping to hear students singing, hammering, and playing musical instruments, all too often there is only silence, shiny equipment hanging on walls, and students completing low-level clerical tasks.

Even the results-obsessed Hattie bemoans too much teacher talk and says schools are still great places to watch teachers work, as he says: 'we want student stars, not teacher stars'. To be fair to Hattie he does make it clear at the beginning of his book 'Visible Learning' that there is more to education than results - and cites citizenship as perhaps the highest outcome.

The OECD 2030 Learning Framework that we have been so indebted too also insists that you can't teach things like creativity or responsibility in a passive way. Students have to develop these attributes actively - or as Nietzsche put it, 'the doer alone learneth'. We can only create activists with active learning and Greta Thunberg has demonstrated that, if we are going to save the planet, then it will probably be through the youth. Our generation has demonstrably failed and so we should encourage students to find their own voices rather than have to sit all day listening to ours. No more power-point by the hour-point!

Rosenshine's 'Principles of Instruction' has become incredibly influential in English schools recently. Rosenshine is great, but the clue is in the title - he sees teachers as instructors and the front cover of Sherrington's book about his work has a massive image of a teacher lecturing the tiny, disembodied heads of her pupils. This suggests children are little more than computers that need inputting with data. There is a lot more to real education than that, as I'm sure Sherrington would acknowledge.

There are two ways to get great results out of students. You can do it through fear, pressure, and endless testing or you can do it through inspiration and truly personalised learning. The latter approach takes more creativity and time but, in an age of a perceived mental health epidemic amongst young people, wouldn't it be better to err on the side of caution and go down this route instead?

We hope you have enjoyed reading about our Fourth Way journey and that it has given you ideas or inspiration for your own interactions with young people - whether you are an educator, parent, or community leader. There is still a tendency in schools to see education as merely the acquisition of knowledge. We love knowledge, but we see it as only the starting point of a real education. Students have to be smarter than their smartphones if they are to compete in the modern world; they need to be good at the things computers aren't - like creativity, problem-solving, and taking responsibility (CPR).

We would like to finish by thanking Andy Hargreaves for his invaluable help and support over the years. 50 years ago Bosworth produced a book called 'School for the Community', edited by our school's first Headteacher, Tim Rogers. We have (in true Fourth Way fashion) tried to build on some of the best practices from our school's innovative past, as well as learn from some of its (inevitable) mistakes. The result is, that thanks to everyone's hard work, we are now a fully-fledged, 21st-century school for the community; we have Andy Hargreaves and the 'The Fourth Way' to thank for that.

Bibliography

1. **The Fourth Way**, Andy Hargreaves and Dennis Shirley, 2009, Corwin.

2. **School for the Community**, edited by Tim Rogers, 1971, Routledge.

3. **Moving**, Andy Hargreaves, 2020, Solution Tree

4. **About Our Schools**, Tim Brighouse and Mick Waters, 2022, Crown House

5. **The Unfinished Revolution**, John Abbot and Terry Ryan, 2001, Bloomsbury

6. **Professional Capital**, Micheal Fullan and Andy Hargreaves, 2012, Teachers College Press

7. **Visible Learning**, John Hattie, 2008, Routledge

8. **The Global Fourth Way**, Andy Hargreaves and Dennis Shirley, 2012, Sage

Appendix - Key documents and displays

Fourth Way Principles poster

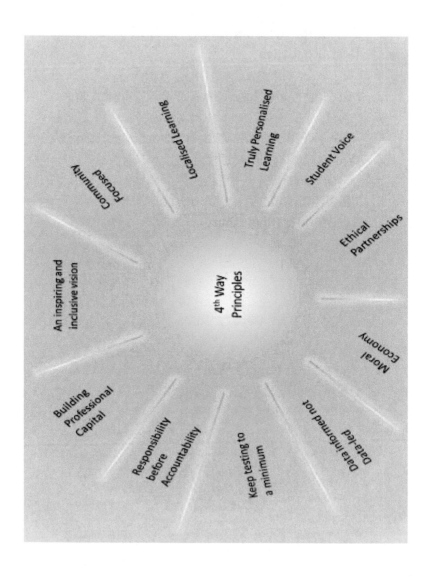

Staffroom display organised around the poster above -
we added to this as we went along

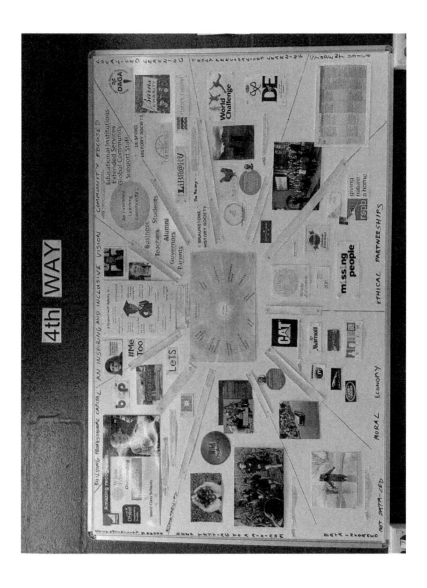

Fourth Way narrative display

Fourth Way Projects 2014-15

Progress	Green	Amber	Red
Cat Pre-Apprenticeship	✓		
Next Pre-Apprenticeship	✓		
Richard III	✓		
Desford Library	✓		
Community Garden	✓		
French Partnership	✓		
Desford FC	✓		
Community Film Studio	✓		
Barns Charity Fields	✓		
Leicester Forest	✓		
Politics/Citizenship	✓		
Henrichment	✓		
Adult Education		✓	
STEM		✓	
Alumni		✓	
Good Neighbours		✓	
Student Voice		✓	
Skateboard Plaza			✓
Staff Well-being		✓	
Lunch-time activities		✓	
Trips and Visits	✓		
SMSC	✓		
Environment	✓		
Cold War	✓		
Impact			
Year 7	✓		
Year 10,11,12,13		✓	
Learning Community	✓		

Framework Adapted from the table in 'The Global Fourth Way', by Andy Hargreaves and Dennis Shirley (8) with the historic Bosworth school logos matched to the 'ways'.

Bosworth Academy and the Fourth Way

		The First Way	The Second Way	The Third Way	The Fourth Way
Pillars of Purpose and Partnership	Purpose	Innovative; Inconsistent	Markets and standardisation	Performance targets; raise the bar, narrow the gaps	Inspiring, inclusive, innovative mission.
	Community	Little or no engagement	Parent choice	Parent choice and community service delivery	Public engagement and community engagement
	Investment	State investment	Austerity	Renewal	Moral Economy
	Corporate Influence	Minimal	Extensive – charters and academies, technology, testing products	Pragmatic partnerships with government	Ethical partnerships with civil society
	Students	Happenstance involvement	Recipients of change	Targets of service delivery	Engagement and voice
Principles of Professionalism	Learning	Eclectic and uneven	Direct instructions to standards and test requirements	Customised learning pathways	Truly personalised; mindful teaching and learning
	Teachers	Variable training quality	Flexible, alternative recruitment	High qualification, varying retention	High qualification, high retention
	Associations	Autonomous	Deprofessionalised	Data driven	Evidence – informed
	Learning Communities	Discretionary	Contrived	Data driven	Evidence – informed
Catalysts of Cohesion	Leaderships	Individualistic variable	Line managed	Pipelines for delivering individuals	Systemic and sustainable
	Networks	Voluntary	Competitive	Dispersed	Community focused
	Responsibility	Local and little accountability	High-stakes; testing by census	Escalating targets, self-monitoring, and testing by census	Responsibility, first, testing by sample, ambitious and shared targets
	Differentiation and Diversity	Underdeveloped	Mandated and standardised	Narrowed achievement gaps and data driven interventions	Demanding and responsive teaching

The Bosworth College
Leicester Lane, Desford
Leicester LE9 9JL
Principal
Timothy Rogers BA
WE CARE

Together We Achieve
To Learn To Achieve
No student will
underachieve
Be better than you
thought you could be

Bosworth Academy

A Learning Community

152

Energy

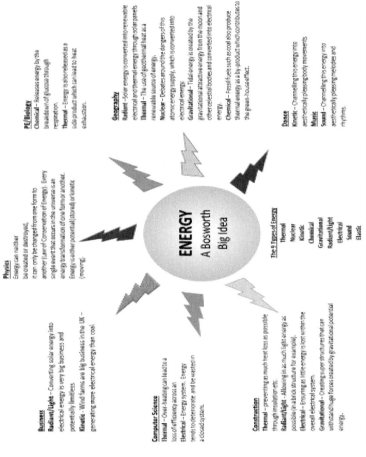

Physics
Energy can neither be created or destroyed, it can only be changed from one form to another (Law of Conservation of Energy). Every single event that occurs in the universe is an energy transformation of one form or another. Energy is either potential (stored) or kinetic (moving).

PE/Biology
Chemical – Release as energy by the breakdown of glucose through respiration.
Thermal – Energy is also released as a side product which can lead to heat exhaustion.

Geography
Radiant – Solar energy is converted into renewable electrical and thermal energy through solar panels.
Thermal – The use of geothermal heat as a renewable source of energy.
Nuclear – Debates around the dangers of this atomic energy supply, which is converted into electrical energy.
Gravitational – Tidal energy is created by the gravitational attractive energy from the moon and other celestial bodies and converted into electrical energy.
Chemical – Fossil fuels such as coal also produce thermal energy as a by-product which contributes to the green-house effect.

Dance
Kinetic – Channelling this energy into aesthetically pleasing body movements.

Music
Sound – Channelling this energy into aesthetically pleasing melodies and rhythms.

ENERGY
A Bosworth Big Idea

The 9 Types of Energy
Thermal
Nuclear
Kinetic
Chemical
Gravitational
Radiant/Light
Electrical
Sound
Elastic

Business
Radiant/Light – Converting solar energy into electrical energy is very big business and potentially limitless.
Kinetic – Wind farms are big business in the UK – generating more electrical energy than coal.

Computer Science
Thermal – Over-heating can lead to a loss of efficiency across an electrical system.
Electrical – Energy system. Energy tends to deteriorate and be wasted in a closed system.

Construction
Thermal – preventing as much heat loss as possible through insulation etc.
Radiant/Light – Allowing in as much light energy as possible (in a brick structure for example).
Electrical – Ensuring as little energy is lost within the overall electrical system.
Gravitational – Creating super structures that can withstand huge forces created by gravitational potential energy.

Everyday application - we make energy transformation decisions all the time, when you turn on a light, turn off a computer, open a window you are deciding whether to save or waste energy. Much of this energy is provided by fossil fuels (chemical energy) which leads to global warming.

Audience

AUDIENCE
A Bosworth Big Idea

IT/Business

Media – Students are required to shape a product to meet the needs of a particular target audience.

Computer Science – Students develop a product in conjunction with feedback from the client via market research.

Business – Understanding the purchasing desire of the clients.

English

Audience and 'reader' are often discussed as one of the same thing.

Effect of a writers craft is the heart of literary analysis and discussion, particularly concerning 'sympathy' or 'antipathy' for characters, creation of audience etc.

How context affects audience perception – modern vs the writer's contemporary Context.

Creating tone (Big Lang) for a particular audience and understanding that affects use of language

Construction

A more viewing the built environment – this can be perceived in many ways, each individual will have a different view, how do we teach students to meet the needs of clients, there are both the audience and the commissioner of the work.

AO1

Intended use of Target Market for a design or product. Types of customers – nutritional needs/allergies etc.

Performing Arts

Creators of performance can be used for art, as well as preparing for live-case performances with the audience.

Performing in front of an audience develops character & audience.

Audience participation means involving the audience within the performance eg pantomime direct address.

Students are worked on how an audience can understand & make meaning of their performance.

Media Studies

Audience is one of our 4 key concepts. We look at how audiences are

Segmented – divided into different categories such as age, gender, class, ethnicity etc.

Targeted – How media texts are constructed to appeal to specific audience categories.

Consumption – how the media texts are received by the target audience in identifying, devices etc.

Active – are audiences passive consumers who are easy to influence and control through the media or are they active consumers who use the media for their own purposes?

PE

The effects of an audience on performance is an A level PE topic. Social facilitation -when an audience help performance.

Social inhibition – when an audience hinders participation.

In general an audience speeds up performance due to an increase in arousal. It also makes it more likely for novices to make mistakes with experts performers are likely to benefit. Other psychological processes their desire to share

- Evaluation apprehension – fear of being judged by an audience
- Distraction/conflict theory – audience interrupts your focus
- Proximity effect – the closer an audience is the stronger the effect.

154

Visual Language

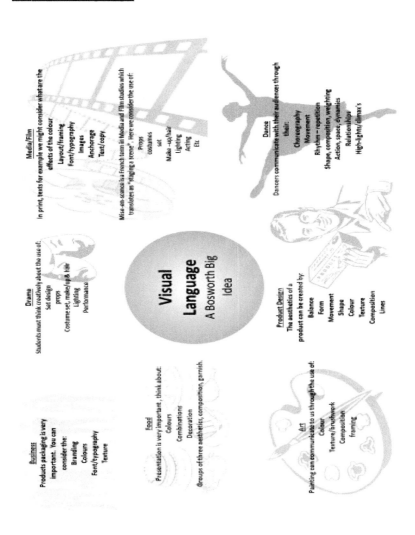

158